# THERE IS MORE

## MIRACLES, VISIONS, COINCIDENCES AND CONVERSIONS

L D Ryan PhD PE

*To Riona from L D Ryan*
*2017.*

1. Copyright © 2015 L D Ryan
2. All rights reserved.
3. ISBN: 1501030876
4. ISBN-13: 9781501030871

# DEDICATION

Since this book is nothing less than what Jesus Christ did in the author's life and others, I want to dedicate the book to Him. With great thanks for coming to someone unfit for His service. I thank you Lord. He sent the Holy Spirit to live, work, and teach within my heart. I am what I am today because of the love of God. Thank you Lord.

# CONTENTS

|  | Acknowledgments | i |
|---|---|---|
|  | Preface | Page 7 |
| Chapter 1 | With My Own Eyes | Page 19 |
| Chapter 2 | Healing in Juarez | Page 31 |
| Chapter 3 | Persecution | Page 33 |
| Chapter 4 | How's it Working | Page 37 |
| Chapter 5 | Miracles and Coincidence | Page 51 |
| Chapter 6 | Judah | Page 65 |
| Chapter 7 | David S | Page 69 |
| Chapter 8 | The Bush | Page 75 |
| Chapter 9 | Truth from the Word | Page 79 |
| Chapter 10 | Finding Sue | Page 83 |
| Chapter 11 | The Greatest Miracles | Page 89 |
| Chapter 12 | Visions | Page 107 |
| Chapter 13 | The Scriptures not Read | Page 119 |
| Chapter 14 | History of the Church | Page 139 |
| Chapter 15 | Closure | Page 167 |

# ACKNOWLEDGMENTS

I am deeply indebted to my wife Susan for the encouragement in writing this book. Finding Sue in Toledo, Ohio was one of the biggest miracles in my life. Sue has helped in the proofing and making the book a little less offensive to readers than it might have been. I thank her for the tedious task of proofing this book. With the Holy Spirit's input, I pray that the reader will sense that God wants more out of this generation in reaching and feeding the lost sheep.

Without apology, I acknowledge the Holy Spirit's input. My goal is to write down some of the miracles in my life to help the readers believe and to go to work for the Lord in reaching the lost. I also want the reader to see the fences that many well meaning denominations have created between them and the Holy Spirit. If there is some problem believing that what happened in the New Testament is available today, I pray there is some real searching of the Bible to verify the truth of His available power. I have included the history of the early church in some of their own words to help the reader understand that the death of the original Apostles did not end miracles and other direct work of the Holy Spirit as is claimed by numerous modern Christians. The modern church, in many cases, does not spiritually compare to the early church. **There is more!** These three words came to me through Julie Roy, and I know she received this Word from the Holy Spirit and passed it on. **There is more!** Open the gate in your life and walk through to a powerful life in Christ leaving the fenced life behind.

I would also like to thank Dr. Mitch Ryan, Judah Ryan and Jack Apple for their very valuable contributions to this book as they shared their own stories of God's work in their lives.

# PREFACE:

Someone said, "Life is what you do while waiting to die." People can go through life unaware of the mysterious components that contribute to their existence. Another person can pass through from birth to death marveling at the mysteries and magic of it all. One believes all the elements of life came from an explosion through evolution. Another believes God created all this for the folks he loves. Some never give it a thought.

The author wants to shine a light on the subject that the Holy Spirit is still at work today as He was in the early church. It makes no sense to eliminate the power of the Holy Spirit in our time that is different but just as challenging.

Or perhaps my imagination working overtime has given the title of miracle to just coincidental happenings. Where did all the stuff of life come from? Was it from God or from a cosmic explosion? Is it a design or an accident? *"**There is more**"* is a book to help the reader decide his or her view of what is happening "out there" in our world.

There are some interesting statements by others that the author has included as a preface to reading the book. A section of Joshua out of the Bible is included because this is what the author is attempting to do. There is a part of our brain that removes some of our memories more or less automatically. I am afraid we would be overloaded with stuff from the past without forgetting some of the events, but I do not want to delete what God has done in my life. In Joshua, the Israelites used a pile of twelve rocks they carried out of the dried up bed in the Jordan River when they crossed at flood stage. Here, the author is using a book instead of a rock memorial.

In a very popular devotional guide by Sarah Young called "Jesus Calling", the September 2$^{nd}$ page seems to fill an opinion held by some Christians. (The capitalized pronouns are God, Jesus, and the

Holy Spirit speaking.)

*"Living in dependence on Me is a glorious adventure. Most people scurry around busily, trying to accomplish things through their own strength and ability. Some succeed enormously; others fail miserably. But both groups miss what life is meant to be: living and working in collaboration with Me.*

*"When you depend on Me continually, your whole perspective changes. You see miracles happening all around, while others see only natural occurrences and coincidences. You begin each day with joyful expectations, watching to see what I will do. You accept weakness as a gift from Me, knowing that My power plugs in most readily to consecrated weakness. You keep your plans tentative, knowing that My plans are far superior. You consciously live, move, and have your being in Me, desiring that I live in you. I in you and you in me ... This is the intimate adventure I offer you"*[i]

## Joshua 4: 2 to18 (KJV)

*"Take you twelve men out of the people, out of every tribe a man, And command ye them, saying, Take you hence out of the midst of Jordan, out of the place where the priests' feet stood firm, twelve stones, and ye shall carry them over with you, and leave them in the lodging place, where ye shall lodge this night.*

*"Then Joshua called the twelve men, whom he had prepared of the children of Israel, out of every tribe a man:*

*"And Joshua said unto them, Pass over before the ark of the LORD your God into the midst of Jordan, and take ye up every man of you a stone upon his shoulder, according unto the number of the tribes of the children of Israel:*

*"That this may be a sign among you, that when your children ask their fathers in time to come, saying, What mean ye by these*

*stones? Then ye shall answer them, That the waters of Jordan were cut off before the ark of the covenant of the LORD; when it passed over Jordan, the waters of Jordan were cut off: and these stones shall be for a memorial unto the children of Israel forever.*

*"And the children of Israel did so as Joshua commanded, and took up twelve stones out of the midst of Jordan, as the LORD spake unto Joshua, according to the number of the tribes of the children of Israel, and carried them over with them unto the place where they lodged, and laid them down there.*

*"And Joshua set up twelve stones in the midst of Jordan, in the place where the feet of the priests which bare the ark of the covenant stood: and they are there unto this day.*

*"For the priests which bare the ark stood in the midst of Jordan, until every thing was finished that the LORD commanded Joshua to speak unto the people, according to all that Moses commanded Joshua: and the people hasted and passed over.*

*"And it came to pass, when all the people were clean passed over, that the ark of the LORD passed over, and the priests, in the presence of the people.*

*"And the children of Reuben, and the children of Gad, and half the tribe of Manasseh, passed over armed before the children of Israel, as Moses spake unto them:*

*"About forty thousand prepared for war passed over before the LORD unto battle, to the plains of Jericho.*

*"On that day the LORD magnified Joshua in the sight of all Israel; and they feared him, as they feared Moses, all the days of his life.*

"And the LORD spake unto Joshua, saying, "Command the priests that bear the ark of the testimony, that they come up out of Jordan. Joshua therefore commanded the priests, saying, Come ye up out of

Jordan.

*"And it came to pass, when the priests that bare the ark of the covenant of the LORD were come up out of the midst of Jordan, and the soles of the priests' feet were lifted up unto the dry land, that the waters of Jordan returned unto their place, and flowed over all his banks, as they did before."[ii]*

The Israelites had a pile of 12 rocks taken out of the middle of Jordan River as a memorial to what God had done. They placed them where they camped that night. They were supposed to tell their children what the Lord had done at this location. It was a reminder to the people that experienced the miracle and to their children's children. Creating a monument is one of the real messages of the miracle, but our minds question how God did this. We get lost in the details of how God took a river in flood stage and held it up while the children of Israel crossed the Jordan.

Assume the men were in close order drill with 6 men per row with 4 feet between the rows. Assume they crossed at 3 miles per hour. The length of the column would be extremely long at 26,667 feet if the 40,000 fighting men crossed as a unit. By multiplying 40,000 by 4 and dividing by 6, the distance is 26,667 feet, which is over 5 miles long. Assume the warriors marched at 3 miles per hour, which is 15,840 feet per hour. Dividing 15,840 into the 26,667 feet gives 1.68 hours to cross.

It took 1.68 hours just to get the warriors across with 6 men abreast and 4 feet between each row in one group. Of course the one group could be multiple groups crossing at the same time, which would change the time to cross. What can be concluded from this simple calculation is it took a long time to get everybody across the Jordan River, which makes the miracle even more spectacular when considering all the adults, children, possessions, and livestock.

For some reason the simpler the miracle the more difficult it is to understand or believe. It took a long time to get all the Israelites across the Jordan River. The missing fact is how wide was the crossing? Did the priests hold the Ark of the Covenant up while the people crossed, or did they get relieved by standby priests, or did they set the Ark on the river bed?

Even though this calculation is probably meaningless, it does give more information about the miracle. The Israelites had the tabernacle with all its components, and they surely had animals, tents, and food supplies. The conclusion is that it took a long time to cross the Jordan. The water was stopped for hours to accomplish the crossing.

Another source of evidence is to look at the people surrounding the miracle. The warriors were extremely pumped when they went on to Jericho, and that was because they just saw a mighty miracle. The Christians of the early church went to their horrible deaths rather than to say a few good words about the emperor and say yes to the Romans' gods. A little white lie would have saved their lives, but they believed so strongly in the Gospel that death didn't sway them. These issues help me believe.

The miracle crossing the Jordan River is the stopping of the water flow at flood stage. The parting of the Red Sea actually seems more possible to the skeptic than does the stopping of water flow of the Jordon River at flood stage.

Basically, the suspension of gravity is the mechanism of the miracle. We know, if you believe Acts 1 in the Bible, God is capable of turning gravity off as 500 witnesses saw Jesus rise up into heaven, assuming his body had mass. In fact, gravity is the glue that causes the theory of evolution to crumble because the mechanism of gravitational pull is unknown and certainly cannot evolve. The equation for gravity is well known, but the fact that the gravitational force is directly proportional to the product of the mass of the object and the mass of the earth divided by the square of the distance between the masses. The gravitational constant "k" is the fudge factor that makes everything true in the equation. This equation doesn't mean humanity knows anything about gravity.

The distance to the sun is another interesting scientific correction. In Grovanni and Richner's day the distance from the earth to the sun was calculated as 86,991,966.9 miles. Today the distance has been recalculated as 92,955,233 miles. Now either one of these two calculation is wrong or the sun and earth are moving away from each other. The calculations were made by shooting the sun to get the angle from two different places on the earth. This gives an angle at each location. Then if the distance is known between the two sites, the distance to the sun can be easily calculated.

I have a son, Dr. Steven Ryan, who needed research from other scientists for his own projects, and he has found that some of this research was flawed and untrue. The author checked one mechanical engineering equation on the torsion of thin walled member and found the material twisted twice what the equation predicted. If the reader is worshiping science, I expect his or her exposure has been limited. Science is not infallible. Men err.

Do I believe in miracles? Yes, yes, yes. That is one of the reasons for the book. This book is my pile of rocks so that my children and I can remember what I believe God has done in my life. Nothing changes with time as far as God is concerned. He is the same yesterday, today, and forever. Not only have I included my personally witnessed miracles, but, I have included other people's coincidences or miracles when they are from reliable sources.

Before we go forth, I need to explain to the reader why there will be controversy in this book. There are three categories of people "out there" and there are subdivisions within the groups. "Out There" is vague and sort of like "they". They said it is going to rain. They are stupid. Basically, "out there" means people without names or faces that are not in the same room or place with the person who says "out there". We heard something from someone "out there".

The three groups "out there" are: Traditionalists, Spirit Filled, and unrepentant Sinners.

The Traditionalists believe in the denomination's doctrine. For reasons that cannot be proven from scripture, miracles supposedly stopped with the death of the Apostles in the minds of some. When Jesus raised Lazarus from the dead, a few of the witnesses ran back to the Pharisees and may have said: "I don't know how he did it, but surely it was a very good trick." They certainly did not believe in the miracle. **(John 11:46)** The conclusion by the Moses' Traditionalists was that they had to kill Jesus according to their belief. Miracles made these folks angry, and the anger still is evident in today's Traditionalist. It basically blows some of their beliefs away, and this makes them feel stupid and invalidates their sacred doctrines. In the New Testament, it was Jesus versus Moses in the minds of the Pharisees. Jesus was a blasphemer, which required the Pharisees to stone Jesus to death according to Moses' Law. Jesus tried to tell them if you don't believe in me, believe in the miracles. Nothing has changed with people today. The author observed so many people that are Traditionalist who fight what is so clearly stated in the Bible.

The Sinners, who are lost and on their way to Hell according to the Christian belief, have nothing to protect or defend like some off-based doctrine coveted by Traditionalists. Their attitude is entirely different from the Traditionalists. The Sinners, in many cases, don't care one way or the other. They may not believe in coincidences or miracles, but they have nothing to defend. They are without doctrine except to: "Look out for number one." Their response to miracles are: "What are you smoking?" Or "that is nice." These folks are much easier to deal with than Traditionalists.

The Spirit Filled group should give the miracle worker a "high five" and believe the miracle came from God. "Should" is the key, and realizing that humans are imperfect, sometimes there is a surprise awaiting where some of the details might not quite fit the Spirit filled person's concept of how the details should be. In a perfect world, a God directed coincidence, vision, or a miracle should be believed by everyone if coming from a reliable source that does not have some ulterior motive. It is up to the reader to scrutinize the Coincidences, Visions, or Miracles.

## *Coincidence:*

The "Webster's New World College Dictionary" defines Coincidence: **"An accidental and remarkable occurrence of events or ideas at the same time, suggesting but lacking a causal relationship."**

## Miracle:

**"An event or action that apparently contradicts known scientific laws and is hence thought to be due to supernatural causes such as an act of God."**

## Vision:

**"Something supposedly seen by other than normal sight; something perceived in a dream, trance, etc. or supernaturally revealed, as to a prophet."** [iii]

Almost everyone can point to a fork in the road, a coincidence that required a decision to go one way or the other, and a clear understanding that the decision changed his or her life forever. Sometimes there is knowledge that the wrong choice was made. What would have happened if I would have married Sue rather than Marie? What would have happened if my son, killed in Afghanistan, would have picked another branch of service or would have gone to college? What would have happened if my daughter would have left the house one minute later where she would have missed the crash that killed her due to the fact that she and the drunk driver got to the intersection at the exact same time? Or is the unpopular statement, from the author's point of view, that "when your number is up, it is up", and there is nothing that a person can do about it? Here is my proof that this concept is untrue.

## Statistics on Deaths per 10,000 vehicles:[iv]

Reading the chart above, there were approximately 27 deaths per 10,000 for vehicles in 1933, and in 2008 the death rate went down to approximately 1 death per 10,000 vehicles. This raises two possibilities. The theory that when your number is up, it is up is wrong, or the angel in heaven is changing the numbering system with time. The real truth is safety works with safer roads and vehicles, fewer people die.

Our goal is to have the reader think and calculate wherever possible to get a handle on the truth. Some things are just too complicated, and there is no way to use tools to check out the miracle or coincidence. That is where faith comes to play. Faith is received from God by prayer, but some people reject the idea of faith. They will try to be good, or they will attend church to play it safe. There is another way that is more intelligent. Generally the people in Christian nations believe that there is a heaven and a hell. Most have tried to protect themselves with insurance. They have health insurance, fire insurance, car insurance, flood insurance, liability insurance and long term care insurance to protect them when they get old. The smart way would be to pick up a little hell insurance by following what the Bible teaches. If the Bible is not true, the dead will be unaware of this. The lights are out and that is all there is to that. Do you remember before you were born? Of course not. From the beginning of time to before you and I were conceived, that is exactly how it will be if there is no heaven, no hell, and no God.

Robert Frost wrote the best support for the importance of decisions in his poem "The Road Not Taken:" The last paragraph of the poem:

***"I shall be telling this with a sigh***

***Somewhere ages and ages hence:***

***Two roads diverged in a wood, and I—***

***I took the one less traveled by,***

***And that has made all the difference."*** [iv]

Decisions are important and literally change our lives. I have heard the statement from many Christians that they believe that God is in charge. This is fine until the nightly news broadcast about a twelve year-old missing girl. The authorities eventually find her decomposed body and conclude that she was raped, tortured, and dismembered by some sex maniac. How did the God of love let that happen? Well maybe it was punishment for the sin of her parents or the girl did something very bad or we blame God in our heart. Or ??????

It is better understood if Christians remember, we are a fallen species, and God has given us free will to do whatever we please down here on earth. In the Lord's prayer, He says to pray that: **"God's will be done on earth as it is in heaven."** Jesus did not come up with a prayer that is not relevant any more. God's will is still not done on this earth. Let's think about pitching the concept that God is in charge here on earth. If he is, free will is gone, and God has some serious charges against Him or Her.

This "preface" has material that should be helpful in the reading of this book. A person can walk through life without serious thought to what is actually happening. Just maybe the preface will get the reader's mind thinking about "There is more" in our faith than what is normally practiced.

The author will likely create controversy and agreement. If the reader is so inclined. The author wants your reactions both positive and negative sent to ldyan1934comment@gmail.com as substance for another edition of this book. Whatever response the reader has, positive or negative, is welcomed. Emails received will be viewed as permission from the sender to publish without any compensation, and agree that it is the author's option to use the email or not in future publications.

All that is asked in reading this book is to look at the miracle and then look at the events surrounding the miracle. A simple calculation brought to light that it took a long time to cross the Jordan River in flood stage for the children of Israel. Being an apostle and disciple around Jesus, and being a Christian during the first two centuries says something. These people believed the gospel with all it signs and wonders such that they would choose to die by wild beast, sadistic instruments, or fire rather than say that Caesar was god. That is evidence of the reality of faith because what surrounded the belief was a positive proof of the truth of Jesus Christ. These followers were more than willing to die for their faith.

***Finally, keep in mind what Jesus said: John 10:37-38 "If I do not the works of my Father, believe me not. But if I do, though you believe***

***not me, believe the works: that ye may know, and believe, that the Father is in me, and I in him."*** (KJV)

This is why miracles still happen so that people will believe in Jesus, and God works in this world through you and me. Miracles help us to do God's business. We pray so that God can communicate with us as we are His workers. Prayer without feet on the ground afterwards is not very effective.     LD Ryan

# CHAPTER 1: WITH MY OWN EYES

## Dad and Mom:

Generally, you get what you get as far as parents are concerned. There is no shopping around or checking their evaluations on the internet. The first and biggest risk a person has is getting parents. There are terrible people who become parents, and there are almost perfect people that become parents. Most lie somewhere between saint and sinner. It would have been nice to have a five star rating system, and I would have had the chance of choosing my parents. I would not have picked my mom and dad because at best they started parenting with a one star rating.

My maternal relatives were night and day different from my paternal relatives. My mother's people were merchants in a small town in northern Indiana. My father's family were hard drinking, and hard fighting Irish who fought in bars and the military. A few were entrepreneurs. My mother's people were inclined to be good citizens and Christian. Dad's were not. Mom was Scottish and Swiss. Dad was Irish and German. If opposites attract, they certainly fit that criteria. Mom was a self conscious introvert and was worried about what other people thought. Dad was outgoing and did not care what people thought. The community did not get a vote in father's life.

My future parents met in my great grandfather's store. Mom gave Dad a free cookie, and dad wanted more. They ran off and got married. My grandfather Ryan saw them sitting together on his porch. Nobody knew they were married. My grandfather asked them if they were married and if they had a place to stay. Yes they were married, and no they did not have a place to stay. Right from the start, they needed help outside themselves to survive.

Doc Ryan, my grandfather took care of them from the beginning. Doc was just a nickname, his formal education was limited. His brother's nickname was Posy because he was once stuck on a dirt road and he pulled weeds and flowers to put under the wheels for traction. When someone saw him with flowers underneath his Model T wheels, the rural community called him Posey. The Ryan clan, for some reason, attracted nicknames.

The Second World War came along and my father and his brother went to war as their relatives did before them. Uncle Bob was on a gunboat in the South Pacific. Dad was a medic landing after the first waves at Normandy. Dad went through France into Germany picking up the wounded.

The military effects people in different ways. Our past wars were fought with men in the field or at sea for long periods of time. Now some fly in for a heavy fire fight and fly out to a secure base. In both cases of long and short term fighting, it produces mental casualties. Many warriors came home with PTS, and alcohol and drugs provided relief. A few have nightmares the rest of their lives. Many in the military experience long periods of boring and uncomfortable living with periods of terrifying action. Available alcohol provided something to do when off the line. Drinking in the military often produced alcoholics after service regardless of the trauma. My dad and uncle both came home from the war as alcoholics. My best friend told me that he never saw my Uncle Bob sober. Bob was drunk for long periods of time. He was a binge drinker. My dad on the other hand was drunk one day and then hung-over the second day. He continued to work every day. My uncle retired at 35 years of age, and he worked only when he needed to buy more booze. Uncle Bob would fight anybody anywhere. He was not selective and lost many a fight. Dad was more selective, and picked his fights carefully.

My dad ,when sober was a nice guy, but he was a mean drunk. Mom was five feet two inches tall, and was more of a fighter than my Dad. She was mean sober, and nice with a few drinks in her, which I rarely saw. When dad was drunk, Mom left him alone most of the time. When he was sober, mom fought him. This resulted in one day dad was drunk causing mayhem, and the next day, mom was fighting her husband causing mayhem. My sister and I lived a chaotic life. We both left home as soon as possible after graduating from high school. In fact we begged our parents to divorce.

One night the fighting reached a climax. Dad was in the process of killing mom. He had her down and was choking her to death. She was turning blue from lack of oxygen. My sister and I were screaming and ready to piss our pants. I knew I had to do something. I went to the closet and got my 410 shotgun. I loaded a round in the chamber, and went back to the potential murder scene. I put the gun in dad's chest and told him to get off mom. He did. When he got up, I still had the gun in his chest. He didn't try to grab the gun. He just pushed on the barrel with his chest and kept saying, "shoot me". He wanted to die, and he was trying to get me to do it. He pushed me back into the bedroom with the cocked gun on his chest. Now, I believe that God intervened even though I was an atheist kid at twelve years-old. I removed the gun from Dad's chest and turned and threw the gun, still cocked, through the bedroom window. My parents stopped fighting and said that I had gone nuts. My parents were two self centered people that didn't know they were raising kids. They didn't know, and they didn't care.

My oldest sister and I had long since left home when we heard that my parents became Christians. Yah sure, I thought. By this time, the family was broken and I basically disliked my not so smart parents. We suffered as children and as a family. Not only did nothing change between my parents and me, but if it were true about their conversion, where in Hades was the Church years ago. I was angry at nominal Christians from that day on with their non-Biblical ways.

I heard what happened from the preacher that finally came to the house. I heard it from other people. Leonard and Dorothy had accepted Christ. The instrument or person that led my parents to Jesus told me that he walked into their house. Pointed a finger at my father and said, "You need Jesus." Dad said, "I know it.", he started to cry. The man invited him to church, but Dad said, "I am an alcoholic. I don't belong in church". The evangelist said, "Jesus can fix that." Jesus did. Dad quit drinking and smoking. He went to church, and became a powerful evangelical that led many to Christ. This, without question, was a miracle. Beyond any rational thinking, how could my father be so changed? My mother became a prayer warrior, and her devotion to Jesus was awesome. My parents went from being very bad people to very nice people practically overnight. Eventually, I could not deny what happened and dad and I forgave each other. He became my best friend. I even began to love my mother who caused half the problems in our home with her belief that she was not going to take anything from my alcoholic father or anybody else.

## *Me:*

Before my parents were saved, I had a life changing experience of my own.

My enlistment was about up from the US Navy. The wooden hulled minesweeper was in dry dock for repairs in Elizabeth City, North Carolina. I may have been the only sailor who owned 35 head of cattle, and they were kept in a 500 acre field near Charleston, South Carolina. I went to Charleston to sell the cattle and then I went back to Elizabeth City to bid a non-serious girlfriend goodbye. I went home to Mongo, Indiana. While I was still in uniform, I went to a basketball game in Brighton, Indiana. My high school team was playing and losing as usual. On the way out of the gym, a woman standing at the door stopped me and introduced herself as my oldest sister's teacher. She told me enough in the brief conversation to indicate she was looking for a boyfriend. We arranged a date. Had I known where our relationship was headed at the time, I would have hit the road and never looked back. Now, I thank the Lord for His election to follow Him. Viewed after the fact, this coincident was actually a disguised miracle. In our frequent dating, she told me in no uncertain terms, that if I were dating her, I was going to church. I was, at the time, an atheist, and I could see no permanent harm in accompanying her to church.

The Evangelical United Brethren church near Howe, Indiana was having a revival. So I went with her to the service. I was cocky, arrogant, and completely disinterested in what was going on around me. I didn't listen to the sermon. I was convinced the people were all a bunch of hypocrites. I found out later, this is a typical feeling by every other lost soul on his or her way to hell. I wanted to get out of there. Finally this evangelist stopped talking. Then he did something that I didn't expect. He asked for raised hands for anyone that needed prayer. Yah, sure. Raise your hands hypocrites I thought. At about that time, the girlfriend, who unknown to me was wanting to create a good Christian husband, elbowed me in the ribs. Let's see, I contemplated, the dude up front wants hands raised for prayer, and I have just been elbowed in the ribs by my girlfriend sitting next to me. I got the message and raised my hand. After all, I don't believe there is a God, and a prayer could not be deadly. "I see your hand young fellow", the preacher yelled out for everybody in the church to hear. The girlfriend practically dragged me to the altar, but what she and I didn't know was that God was going to enter the scene. Jesus loved me enough to send an angel or something. This wasn't the girlfriend or flesh and blood member of the congregation or the preacher. This was a vision of something hanging off to the left side of the globe light hanging down from the ceiling. This angel was wearing what looked like peasant clothes. The cloth looked like a course weave similar to burlap. The being or angel had straight brown hair that was almost shoulder length with bangs. The eyes were brown and they stared at me. There was no conversation between the two of us. I don't remember hands or feet. The result was that I believed in the spirit world right then and there, and I was in a mode of repentance. I found out later that this was a vision. It was vivid, and I never forgot it.

Had there been water and had I known what Jesus wanted, I would have been baptized. I was genuinely repentant of my sins. If someone would have asked me if I were "saved", I would not have known what "saved" was. All I knew was that I had seen something like an angel, without wings, and I was really sorry for my sins. I experienced what I found out later was the baptism of repentance. I was sorry for what I had done in general. There was not one big sin that I could recall, but I knew I could not stand in the presence of a holy God. The tears flowed and I believed.

The girlfriend tried to disciple me after that. Our dates were Bible studies. It all helped to catch me up ,the non-churched guy, with the rest of the congregation. At first, I could not find Matthew in the Bible. I was one ignorant repentant guy. By the way, we broke up later. Her task was to lead me to Jesus and with that finished, we were finished.

Years later I realized that I saw a vision in that church. No one came up to me and said, "Did you see that angel hanging up near the ceiling?" Later in my Christian life, I had other vivid visions. It is just a picture and I have had little trouble in interpreting the meaning of the visions. It took years to analyze the happening in the winter of 1955 when I was converted.

***Joel 2:28 And it shall come to pass afterward, that I will pour out my spirit upon all flesh; and your sons and your daughters shall prophesy, your old men shall dream dreams, your young men shall see visions:[vi]***

The scripture of Joel 2:28 that says your daughters shall prophesy should silence the critics of women speaking in church since prophesy is done in church.

My wife has spiritual dreams but I have visions. The next vision was of a beautiful landscape with the frame of a rotting door jam hanging in between me and the scene. There was just the door jam with the lower left rotted away. I told my oldest missionary doctor son about the vision, and he had found the picture that he liked and saved it long before my vision. A scene similar is shown next:

I immediately knew what the vision meant. I was supposed to quit working on secular projects and focus on the Lord's work. The scripture related to this vision was:

***2 Peter 3:10-12** "But the day of the Lord will come as a thief in the night; in the which the heavens shall pass away with a great noise, and the elements shall melt with fervent heat, the earth also and the works that are therein shall be burned up. Seeing then that all these things shall be dissolved, what manner of persons ought ye to be in all holy conversation and godliness, Looking for and hasting unto the coming of the day of God, wherein the heavens being on fire shall be dissolved, and the elements shall melt with fervent heat?"* (KJV)

My engineering degrees and experience allowed me to start businesses or invent machines. The Lord knew that I could be side tracked easily. His will was to have me dedicate almost every waking hour to the building of His kingdom. He also gave me **Acts 20:24,** which says: "*But none of these things move me, neither count I my*

***life dear unto myself, so that I might finish my course with joy, and the ministry, which I have received of the Lord Jesus, to testify the gospel of the grace of God."*** (KJV)

The vision of the beautiful scene with the rotten old door supported the fact that He wanted me to create spiritual things that would not get burned up in the end of time. I am 80 years old. Even though I followed the Bible in witnessing and leading people to my Savior, It was about time to get moving with more intensity.

I had experienced the baptism of repentance way back in the winter of 1955. I knew there was a God and a spiritual world. But for years, Christianity was something I did when I had some spare time. I attended church sporadically. I refrained from getting drunk. I didn't really enjoy sin anymore, but basically, I was like so many other people attending church. I had one foot in the river that flows from the throne of God, and one foot in the world.

I met my soul mate in Toledo, Ohio and we were married. I had not finished my engineering degree at that time. Sue was an RN and readily employable. She, the GI bill, and the rooming house we bought on campus put me through engineering college.

After we were married I quit my drafting job at Dana Corporation and went back to college at Trine University where I finished my Bachelor of Science in Mechanical Engineering. We came out of Angola, Indiana with one son and a wife pregnant with twin sons, and a degree in mechanical engineering.

I worked as an engineer and provided for my family of one wife and three sons. We eventually bought a farm near Kansas, Ohio. I farmed part time and worked as a project engineer for Union Carbide.

An old farmer and his wife who lived across the road invited us to church. It was there in a prayer meeting that I rededicated my life to

Christ. The Holy Spirit came in and we, the Holy Spirit and I, started cleaning house over a period of time.

There were a series of spiritual encounters over the next few years that changed me from a church attendee to a serious evangelist. Due to my experience as a child, I was aware of the suffering of individuals and families outside of the Lord, and I knew what the Holy Spirit could do for them. I also was aware of what the church was not doing, and I had my dad's attitude that I did not care one little bit about what people thought. I cared deeply about what Jesus thought. This attitude will help overcome any embarrassment about the process of evangelism of one on one. Every church that I attended, I started an outreach program. Some pastors joined in and some thought I had some other motivation. I had more fights over evangelism than I did in bar room brawls. I could rarely find anyone, including pastors, who were interested in getting out in the highways and hedges to find His lost sheep. The old established Christians would say they were something else besides evangelists such as teachers or helpers or something. This, of course, is buffalo chips. The only people that I could get to shut off the TV and get out into the world were the converted bums. My definition of bums is anyone who gets with the program of sinning regardless of their social or educational standing. Jesus said he wished us to be either hot or cold. Luke- warm would not do. There are way too many lukewarm people in the church today.

If no one else could see the miracle that Jesus did in my life, I could. If they would have been present in the barroom brawls I started, or listened to my cussing, or saw the other unmentionable things I did, they too would believe in my miraculous conversion. I am truly amazed at the power of conversion and the filling of the Holy Spirit in the lives of people. Sinning can be a blast. Doing what you want whenever you want to is very cool. Living for number one, you would seem to get the best results. Throw the first punch because it may be the only shot you have. Wine, woman, and song given up for Christ is the side issue of my miracle of conversion. Why would the author give up the so called good life for becoming a Christian? Because being a Christian is very awesome. Doing what Frank Sinatra sings about "Doing it My Way" pales in comparison to being filled with the love of God and loving people and doing it His way. God, Jesus, and the Holy Spirit make their abode in the heart of this ex-sinner. I can be in church when our band strikes up songs of joy and literally dance and worship in the Spirit. King David would dance before the Lord and his wife watching was totally turned off. I know what it is to get in sync with the Holy Spirit in worship. I have never been so joyous as when I am worshiping the One that came and rescued me from hell on earth and the hell of Hell.

# CHAPTER 2: HEALING IN JUAREZ

Juarez, Mexico was where I personally saw a women who was blind in one eye healed, a five year-old speak for the first time, and an entire gang saved who were in the service to hurt and rob the Americans.

A Mexican American named Justo C was our translator and the main speaker that eventful night in the early 1980's. There was much emotional drama in the service that night. My son Dan, Justo C, a pastor from Arkansas, and I were up front praying for those in need of prayer. A Mexican woman came up who had one brown eye and the other milky eye that was obviously blind. She asked us to pray for her sightless eye. We laid hands on her and began to pray for healing of her left eye as I recall. Part way into the prayer, she let out a spine chilling scream and took off running around the interior of the church praising the Lord. After a long time of her running and praising the Lord, she came back up front. Justo gave her the microphone and she began in Spanish to ask the congregation to forgive her for her emotional outburst, She was Catholic and not used to doing what she just did in this protestant church. She told the congregation that she could now see out of her blind eye! With her eye restored she left the front and sat down.

Another woman stood up and came up front. A young child was with her. The lady said that her son had never talked, and I guessed the boy was about four or five years old. Could we pray for the healing of his speech? That we did. The prayer went on for some time. There was no outward sign that anything happened. After we finished, she lingered for a short moment. Justo thought she had something to say. She was holding her son in her arms. When the microphone got near her, the boy moved his mouth closer to the microphone and started to talk. There was another emotional scene, but somewhat subdued compared to the healing of a blind eye.

At that point, the gang of men and women were being affected by the miracles happening. They started to pray and worship. They were in a group at the back of the church on the left. The band picked up the tempo, and tears flowed as gang members worshipped and danced before the Lord. They came there to hurt us. They left the church as our brothers and sisters.

We were building a church and our group was tired and stayed back at the motel. Four of us decided to go that night anyway, and we were treated to very impressive miracles. The four of us talked about what happened, and how glad we had not chosen to stay with the others of our work party.

# CHAPTER 3: PERSECUTION

I saw two more significant miracles after the persecution that I experienced for my evangelical inclinations. I shared some of my victories that happened in Arkansas with a Saturday morning men's fellowship in Michigan. I wanted to do what the Lord of the Bible commanded us to do and share with these Christian men the victories in Jesus. These men were from the Traditionalists' camp. There were two other men there that followed the teaching presented in the Bible. I had a bunch of victorious stories to share with the group. Instead of rejoicing in the victories I experienced, some of these men got angry. I must have made some of them feel uncomfortable because I told stories about miracles and conversions. I was confused. Didn't I just share about people who I led to the Lord? Andrew did what I did by leading his brother Peter to the Lord. Or the women at the well did what I did by going to the town and telling people to come and see the Lord who told her everything she had done. They even objected to the idea of leading people to the Lord. Somehow these poor lost sheep were supposed to find the Lord on their own without my leading them.

While many of these Traditionalists were getting "traditionalized" in their churches, I was reading the Bible. Miracles, healings, prophecy, tongues, and many other gifts were there. I believed the gifts were available to all believers. Why not?

Before this episode, I attended a church that wanted to stay inside the church walls and pray. I wanted to pray also, but apparently in my prayers offered to the Lord, I said things like "Lord help me to get outside of the four walls of this church and minister to the lost", which I was doing. One of the assistant ministers called me aside and said, " I have something against you." Our encounter was brief and subdued in church, but he came to one of my businesses and got in my face for being evangelical. He claimed to witness more than I did. He claimed that I did not pray, and he prophesied that he saw someone like me who would suffer without help from the Lord. Finally, he was so angry that he said, "I did not give a s---" I didn't get angry, but I could not help but smile a little. This perfect person just said the "s" word. How un-cool was that?

The senior pastor supported this guy, and he would pass on any comments I made about this encounter I had with the assistant pastor.

The senior pastor and I did visitation. After the confrontation with the assistant pastor, I looked for a place where I could be evangelical without suffering at the hands of the Traditionalists. However, the senior pastor and most of the church were solidly based in the whole Bible.

I went from that church in Arkansas to one meeting in a bar where the senior pastor is very evangelical. He came out of a hurtful church situation and catered to people that had been hurt by the typical church. This church has a high percentage of people that are homeless. The goal of the church is to reach the lost and to help the addicts get free of their demons.

My wife of 57 years and I are classified as snow birds; We live on an island in the middle of Lake Michigan in the summer and Arkansas in the winter. We have two churches that we attend. The church on the island is very traditional, and the pastor is a Traditionalist. We have a Saturday morning men's breakfast where there is a Bible study and discussion. Apparently, my evangelical zeal again caused the Traditionalists problems. The pastor made the comment that he wished that a friend and I would not come to the men's fellowship on Saturday morning. I was hurt, but I could do what he wanted. I wondered if two churches had a problem with my evangelical passion, maybe I was the problem.

As I was driving into town thinking about the Saturday men's fellowship , I was playing the radio. I was listening to NPR music when NPR radio faded and another broadcast came out of the speakers. There was a speaker on the radio, and he said, "If what you are doing is right, keep on doing it." The NPR music came back, and I was slightly shaken by this event. Is this from the Lord? Is this just some coincidence? It certainly was a welcome statement, as I was depressed over what was happening. Rejection is not without pain.

Shortly after that, I was going to take a shower. I usually play music while showering. I skimmed my I-pod menu. I saw something new on my I-pod that I had not put there. Where did this come from I wondered? The person's name was Ray Comfort. I thought he must be a folk singer or country singer. How did this CD get on my I-pod? I didn't put it there. So I played Ray Comfort as I took a shower. The reader can go to the computer and search the name "Ray Comfort" and hear what I heard. There was no singing coming out of Ray Comfort, but it was exactly parallel to my understanding of the Bible. It was confirmation that my approach to evangelism was right on target. Two witnesses, the broadcast and the Ray Comfort CD on my I-Pod, confirmed that I was doing what God wanted me to do. All I was doing was following the Bible. All my critics were following their tradition, which earned them the title of Traditionalists.

# CHAPTER 4: HOW'S IT WORKING

Let's see how the Traditionalists are doing. If it is so beneficial to follow the denomination traditions, what is happening in the world? How is the Gospel doing following the concepts of what the modern church is doing?

The biggest wart on the nose of the modern church is to view the countries around the Mediterranean Sea and beyond. That is where the Gospel of the New Testament started. Paul, in his writing, was always worried about the churches he started of falling away. I wonder what Peter, Paul, John, Philip, Stephen, Ananias, Barnabas, and many others would say if they found out the whole region they gave their lives for is now solidly Muslim?

| Country | % Muslim |
|---|---|
| Afghanistan | 99.8 |
| Albania | 82.1 |
| Algeria | 98.2 |
| Azerbaijan | 98.4 |
| Bangladesh | 90.4 |
| Egypt | 94.7 |
| Gambia | 95.3 |
| Guinea | 95.3 |

| | |
|---|---|
| Indonesia | 88.1 |
| Iran | 99.7 |
| Iraq | 99.7 |
| Jordan | 98.8 |
| Kosovo | 91.7 |
| Kuwait | 86.4 |
| Lebanon | 59.7 |
| Libya | 96.6 |
| Morocco | 99.9 |
| Niger | 98.3 |
| Oman | 87.7 |
| Pakistan | 96.4 |
| Qatar | 77.5 |
| Saudi Arabia | 97.1 |
| Senegal | 95.9 |
| Somalia | 98.6 |
| Tajikistan | 99.0 |
| Tunisia | 99.8 |
| Turkey | 98.6 |

| United Arab Emirates | 76.0 |
| Uzbekistan | 95.6 |
| Western Sahara | 99.6 |
| Yemen | 99.0 |

From the point of view that Christianity started in some of these countries, it looks like a failure to maintain Christianity. When the details of Islam are known and compared to Christianity, it is hard to justify. Women are second class citizens who are often uneducated. Many of things that Islam supports would result in a felony for people in western civilizations. Hollywood and their immoral teaching movies have not helped the relationship between Christian and Muslim. True Christianity does not follow the Hollywood example.

The point is simply this, Islam won where Christianity started. Ask why. There were some mitigating factors such as less tax on Muslims and a military approach to conversion to name a few. The real reason is evangelism in Traditional Christian churches is essentially non-existent.

Looking a little further, the political evolution in the United States is alarming. People are collecting welfare, disability, and food stamps at a shocking rate of increase. This has created a number of Americans that choose not to work even if and when jobs are available. Jobs are sent overseas where people work hard for less money. In certain industries where hard physical work is required, typical Americans are at a disadvantage.

There is a spiritual component to workers that shows up in attitude, sobriety, thankfulness, and integrity. With churches on every other corner, evangelism could change the workforce in America, but it hasn't. We have gone from the greatest generation that came through the Great Depression and World War II to what we have today. What part did the churches have in this decline?

One side note is today's volunteer military. It proves that all is not lost. These are Americans that act like Americans. They are tough disciplined men and women. If a majority of Americans were like today's military, our political failures would be behind us. The majority of Americans are voting for the people that give them the most handouts. Likewise, many churches are serving the people with a watered down gospel that does not require people to be engaged in evangelical outreach. They will stay inside the church building and pray that God will do something. I believe in prayer, but not to the extent of hiding out in the monastery.

## Divorce

There are more social trends that most agree are now happening. Divorce is a serious problem from the Biblical perspective. There are people out there that should never get married. Sometimes, the innocent marry people so screwed up that it is impossible to not divorce. However, there is the scripture related to divorce that we must accept:

**Matthew 5:32 "But I say unto you, That whosoever shall put away his wife, saving for the cause of fornication, causeth her to commit adultery : and whosoever shall marry her that is divorced committeth adultery ".**(KJV)

According to Infographic, an online site, 50% of all marriages end in divorce. The statistics are concise, but the author has not verified the results that Infographic has published on divorce. Here are their conclusions:

## Top 5 reasons people get divorced:[vii]

- Poor communication
- Finances
- Abuse
- No longer attracted to one another
- Infidelity

## Less Likely to get divorced if:

- It's your first marriage
- Your parents are still married
- You are over the age of 25
- You went to college
- You live in a blue state
- You are an atheist

Note, if you are an atheist you are more likely to not get a divorce. What does that say about today's traditional church? Note, blue states have typically thought to have fewer Christians.

## More likely to get divorced if :

- One or both of you are smokers
- One person does all the chores
- You hang out with divorced people
- You met in a bar
- You have a daughter instead of a son
- You have money problems

Here is another interesting but logical fact that can be created in an equation form. Mathematicians could create an equation where the percentage of people getting divorced after a number of divorces multiplied by a proportionality constant could be determined before hand.

where k is the proportionality constant and N is the number of times the person has been divorced. Percent of divorce equals the constant "k" times the number of times "N" the person has been married.

## From the infographic site:

## Divorce Rate:

    41% of 1$^{st}$ marriages end in divorce

    60% of 2$^{nd}$ marriages end in divorce

    73% of 3$^{rd}$ marriages end in divorce

It appears the traditional church has not impacted marriage in any positive way. It is, perhaps, unfair to totally blame the church. Factors such as government handouts, the Supreme Court ruling on same sex marriage, and Hollywood's movie teaching and influencing the movie goers to copy what they see on film.

## Crime

The following graph is derived from FBI statistics for violent crimes:

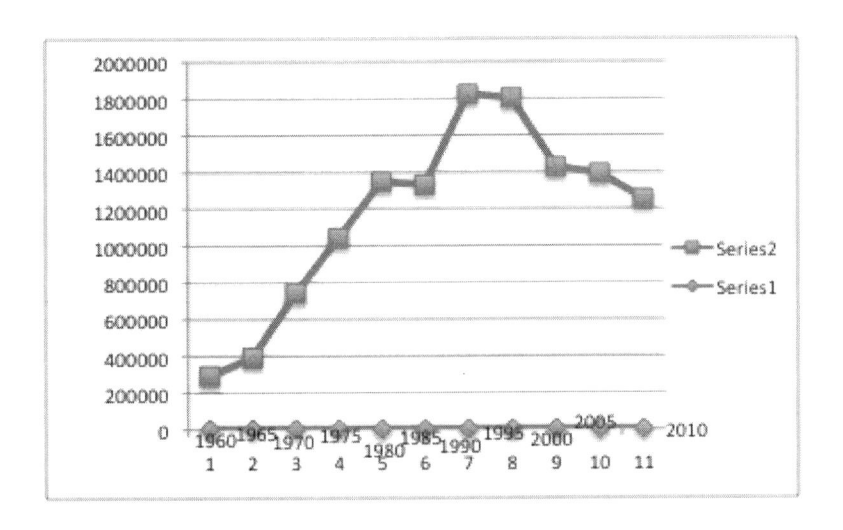

It is quite obvious that the increasing crime rate could reflect, in part, on the non-evangelical stance of the church. Solid Christians do not commit crimes. From 1993 to 2012, there was a decrease from 1,926,017 to 1,214,464 violent crimes, which looks good if the definition of violent crimes was not changed. Basically, crime is increasing every year up to 1993. Then it declined, but there is a good bet somebody changed the definition of violent crime.

Maybe it would be apropos to blame presidents. I am ,of course, being facetious, but it is interesting anyway. JFK reigned from 1961 to 1963; Lyndon Johnson from 1963 to 1969; Richard Nixon from 1969 to 1974; Gerald Ford from 1974 to 1977; Jimmy Carter from 1977 to 1981; Ronald Reagan from 1981 to 1989; George H Bush from 1989 to 1993; Bill Clinton from 1993 to 2001; George W Bush from 2001 to 2008, and finally Obama from 2008 to 2017. If it is not fair to blame presidents then maybe it is not fair to blame the inactive church either.

## Church Service:

One of the big problems, in what we call church, is how we conduct a service. Many churches have 3 hymns, 1 special, responsive reading, and 1 sermon given by the pastor. The sermon could be short or long. It could be interesting or boring. For the older Christians, they often have heard the same sermon before. The people are mute. They sit and listen. It is basically a one or two man show. The audience is supposed to stay awake, sit still, and shut up. I wonder what would happen to my engineering students if they never practiced what I preached at the University?

Since we are always going back to the Bible to guide us in our conduct in life, particularly in the church, it seems logical that we should follow the way to conduct church from the Bible. Why have we not followed what Paul said?

*1 Corinthians 14:1-51 "Follow after charity, and desire spiritual gifts, but rather that ye may prophesy. For he that speaketh in an unknown tongue speaketh not unto men, but unto God: for no man understandeth him; howbeit in the spirit he speaketh mysteries. But he that prophesieth speaketh unto men to edification, and exhortation, and comfort. He that speaketh in an unknown tongue edifieth himself; but he that prophesieth edifieth the church. I would that ye all spake with tongues, but rather that ye prophesied: for greater is he that prophesieth than he that speaketh with tongues, except he interpret, that the church may receive edifying."(KJV)*

*"1 Corinthians 14:26-33 "How is it then, brethren? when ye come together, every one of you hath a psalm, hath a doctrine, hath a tongue, hath a revelation, hath an interpretation. Let all things be done unto edifying. If any man speak in an unknown tongue, let it*

*be by two, or at the most by three, and that by course; and let one interpret. But if there be no interpreter, let him keep silence in the church; and let him speak to himself, and to God. Let the prophets speak two or three, and let the other judge. If any thing be revealed to another that sitteth by, let the first hold his peace. For ye may all prophesy one by one, that all may learn, and all may be comforted. And the spirits of the prophets are subject to the prophets. For God is not the author of confusion, but of peace, as in all churches of the saints".* (KJV)

If the reader has skipped reading the above scripture, go back and read it. Basically Paul is telling us how to hold church. Does it look like today's church? Not at all. Prophesy is the key and we don't know much about it.

Prophecy is found in the church at Rome (Romans 12:6), at Corinth (1Corinthians 12:10), at Ephesus (Eph. 4,11), at Thessalonica (1Thess. 5:20).

## Prophesy:

*Definition from Wikipedia: "Prophecy is a process in which one or more messages that have been communicated to a prophet[1] are then communicated to others. Such messages typically involve divine inspiration, interpretation, or revelation of conditioned events to come (cf. divine knowledge). The process of prophecy especially involves reciprocal communication of the prophet with the (divine) source of the messages. Throughout history, clairvoyance has commonly been used and associated with prophecy."*[viii]

From the author's experience, I had a vision of an old fence with rectangular wire. There was dead grass in the fence indicating that the fence had been there a long time. This happened right before I went to a cottage church. I shared this as something the Lord wanted the group to hear. As I looked around at the small number of people there I knew what the vision meant. All the people in the group were trapped in their lives with a "fence" stopping them from being whole and healed. I don't even want to mention enough details that these very same people will someday read this book and relate it to them. Basically, the vision was something that I shared with the group about fences stopping them in their quest for a better life. What I define as a prophet's message is something that comes from the Holy Spirit that relates to the people's lives. In most cases, It is a positive statement of the Holy Spirit's message about something that can free the hearers from their problems.

The point is that the typical church service today is so far off track when compared to the first century church where prophecy was a vital part of the service. A broad base of involvement in the worship is the key to getting people in being the church outside the four walls.

If you read 1 Corinthians 14 and keep reading, you will run into the very controversial statement made by Paul.

***(1 Corinthians 14:34)2 "Let your women keep silence in the churches: for it is not permitted unto them to speak; but they are commanded to be under obedience, as also saith the law."*** (KJV)

Aside from the scripture **John 14:26** that states that the Holy Spirit will *..."teach you all things"...* where I believe I have been taught that women have a role to speak and share in our meetings. I believe the women in the Corinthian church were unique and needed to be silent."[ix]

In other scripture, Philip the evangelist had four virgin daughters

---

that prophesied. **Acts 21:9 "And the same man had four daughters, virgins, which did prophesy."** When you prophesy you stand up in church, open your mouth, and tell what the Holy Spirit has put on your heart. That is not keeping women silent. The Traditionalists are great at grabbing one scripture and making it one of their articles of faith. Women speak on in churches!

Finally, there is no more separation between the genders on any other category:

**Galatians 3:28: "There is neither Jew nor Greek, there is neither bond nor free, there is neither male nor female: for ye are all one in Christ Jesus."**(KJV)

The Bible definitely puts women on an equal status as men. In fact it looks like it is just fine for women to speak in church. How about the denomination creators? Unity was important to our founding fathers. Yet church leaders took some limited scriptures and created a denomination, which is an act that creates division. A thorough reading of the Bible would stop some of the nonsense that has gone on in the church. However, unfortunately the controversy about women was an issue in the first and second century. It is hard to believe that women did not have a right to vote in the United States until after August 26, 1920 when the constitution was amended.

*"The moment was judged to have come about 170 AD when Montanus, a successful charismatic who described himself as the Paraclete, was declared an enemy of the Church. Many of his closest followers were women, and they clearly played an outstanding role in his movement – as, indeed, they did in one of two of the Pauline congregations. Montanus was attacked by his enemies for breaking up marriages and then giving these inspired matrons ,who flocked to join his ecclesiastical offices. Montanism, or rather the efforts to combat it, played a conclusive role in persuading the orthodox to ban the ministry of women. Tertullian, while still an orthodox propagandist, snarled at this subversion of Church order: 'The*

*impudence of the heretics' women! They dared to teach, to dispute, to carry out exorcisms, perform cures –perhaps they even baptize..."*[x]

Women have had their fair share of bad deals. Ninety five years ago women in the United States got the right to vote. In 1920, the 19th amendment to the Constitution gave them the right to vote. Can you believe that? The Supreme Court ruled against them in 1875, which was predictable based on other decisions of the Supreme Court that gave slave owners the right to have slaves, outlawed prayer in school, allowed mothers to kill unwanted babies, allowed pornography to be distributed, and now are for same sex marriage.

The only reason that women suffrage became a reality is because women were willing to go to prison to get the right to vote. They were arrested and sent to prison. When people go along to get along, the good tends to go from good to bad. If there is one point to this entire book, it is to, at least, think about what has transpired in the modern church and do something about it.

The fact that organizations have a tendency to go downhill after the founding fathers have passed becomes so repeatable that it could be considered a natural law. After Sam Walton died American made products left the shelves of Walmart for products made in China. It was a good temporary solution for low prices, but the payment for this decision will become part of the reason for the demise of America. The American government grows every year by adding paper pushers to their payroll. These creators of paper, forms, and regulations remove people from building long termed infrastructure as an example. The paper may last for one day and then stored to never be used again. What a waste of people power to not create something good and lasting.

The church of Jesus Christ has gone through the same expected decline. In the first and second centuries, Christians died for their faith rather than worship the Roman Emperor and its gods, which would have saved their lives. Christian still die today for their faith, but there is no easy option to save their lives like in the beginning church where they could save their lives with words except for the recent shooting in Oregon. Allegedly the young people who said they were not a Christian took a bullet in the leg. The Christian who did not deny being a Christian took a bullet in the head.

Something has happened to the modern church that appears to be the typical decline in the faith after Jesus went to be with the Father. This decline would be expected in some modern organizations, but it should not be in the faith of the followers of Jesus Christ. He is the same yesterday, today, and forever. When I studied the history of the church, I concluded that I am not sure that I can compare myself to our brothers and sisters that faced fire and beast for their faith. Our prayer should be to grow up in Christ to where we could do what the early Christians did. Without the power of the Holy Spirit inside us, we will be that weak, bench warming, do nothing Christian.

Our problem is that the government of the United States is slowly doing the same thing to today's Christians, but they are doing it slowly one step at a time. Our generation seems to go along to get along. The moves are subtle. The slow immoral changes are: legalizing pornography, legalizing gambling, legalizing marijuana, legalizing abortions, legalizing same sex marriages, and the Supreme Court will legalizing the next thing to destroy American culture.

# CHAPTER 5: MIRACLE OR COINCIDENCE

Sometimes what appears as a coincidence is actually a miracle. While involved in writing this book, I received an email from my son who is an MD and has devoted his life to people in need of medical treatment in countries where there is no medical help. I have known my son from his first breath in the delivery room until now. His whole life could be considered a series of coincidences or an ongoing miracle by the Lord himself. It started on the farm where he was faced with unstructured problems that he or his four brother had to solve singlehanded. I was pretty much like most fathers. I didn't have a clue how to raise a bunch of boys. For some reason, I went through this time in my life where I was a full time professor in engineering and a part time farmer at nights and weekends. It was just coincidental that I had two farms and too much work to handle alone. Or was it? I turned to my sons and we all worked too hard. What I didn't know then was the farm was the training ground for my sons.

I taught engineering for 22 years. Because of my hands-on approach to life, I became good at applying what I learned. The result was that I eventually taught the capstone engineering design course where my students had a senior design project to finish in two semesters. Something that ultimately became clear to me was that farm kids did the best job on their projects. Entrepreneurs' young men were a close second. Some of the typical kids from the city couldn't seem to move the project along. I went from receiving a ridiculously low amount of money for each project from the university to getting real jobs from industry where they paid for the materials that could run into the thousands of dollars. This required some results. I hated to teach the course because I had to push so many young men that I am sure I was the most disliked professor in the college. They either came to me with a farm background or they didn't. The farm kids moved on their projects because they were used to having unstructured problems. The others often had to have everything laid out for them with a few exceptions.

When my boys were young, I had a desire to farm. When they left home and I became older, I wouldn't own a farm if I had to farm it myself. I can treat this as a coincidental event or was it a training ground for my sons? Was it something miraculous to own a farm when the kids were growing up? I now know the benefit of the farm in their lives. Given the fact that my kids can tackle an unstructured problem and take it to completion in good order came from the farm experience. I now think this was a God directed act and not some coincidence.

There was another event that happened that gave my MD son a direction in his life that has made all the difference in so many other people's lives. Was this a divine encounter, a miracle, or just some lucky accident that fell into the coincidence category?

It was snowing hard in Michigan to the point where any sensible person would have turned around and went back home. We always went to church. My wife stayed home because some of our children didn't feel well. I took my oldest son, and we headed for the Sunday night service at our church 20 miles away. For some reason, I turned and went to church not far from the farm. I was not sure of the time of service or exactly where it was. I knew approximately that it was west of Schoolcraft, Michigan. I pulled into the parking lot of this church. We were right on time.

The pastors usually kept a tight guard on the pulpit. He did, however, allow this missionary doctor to speak. We went in, and I expect we sat in the back. An email from my fifty six year old doctor son said we sat on the left. I remember little about what the doctor said, but my young son was mesmerized by the message of the missionary doctor. When we got into the car to head back home, he said, "Dad that is exactly what I want to do. I want to help people who are sick or hurt." From that time on he set his face like a flint in becoming a doctor. This 9 or 10 year old boy kept at what he had to do to become an MD until I went to his graduation from medical school. Was this a coincidence? Or was this part of a miracle with God moving the chess pieces to get His will accomplished?

Another coincidence happened when a person spoke at our church. Tony A ran across the United States. Later in conversation, my son shared his desire to be a doctor. Tony A. told him to go to Wheaton College near Chicago because they had a very good premed program. He did and that made all the difference for him getting into medical school at Wayne State in Detroit.

For ten years my son and his family were in Pakistan up in the Himalaya Mountains where he removed cataracts from totally blind people. He had thousands of successful operations where blind people could see again. Because of the many blind patients, he had time to only fix one eye.

The terrorists tried to kill kids at the Murray Christian School in Pakistan. Two of the children were my grandsons. It was raining that day of the attack so that the kids were inside. This was probably a miracle. If they would have been outside, many children would have died. There were six of the staff killed, and the children were physically unharmed. This attack caused the school to move to another country. Eventually, my son moved to a place near his family. He went to a church and there just happened to be a person there from a bordering country that expressed the need for blankets. What he found was an area in the jungle that had no doctors or hospitals. It was dangerous because there was a war of ethnic cleansing. My farm boy went to work and started a medical training hospital.

There were a number of miracles that produced a doctor to create a medical training facility in the jungle in a war zone. The farm training; the unscheduled stop at a church in a snow storm to hear the presentation of a missionary doctor; an across the US runner who told us about Wheaton College for premed and many more miracles put my son as the founder of the "Jungle School of Medicine". Following is an email my son sent to me as I was writing this book.

From a native five year old boy and his father's point of view in this following story out of the deep jungle, this was a miracle. The father of his sick child didn't know what went into having my son there with the needed equipment. The equipment and the doctor were there when needed. The sick boy's father was not aware of the details that looked like a coincidence that the doctor would be at the hospital soon after a two day hike in the pouring rain. Not only the timing variable of the walk into the hospital, but the doctor just returned from the United States, which was a very big time variable.

My doctor son sent this story on email from the jungle. The sensitive information has been blacked out to prevent problems from the military of this country.

## A Healing

"Almost every time I do my month long rotation of medical teaching at the Jungle School of Medicine (███), I end up with a case that is way over my head. This time, he was already waiting for me before I even arrived. A stoic 5 year old ███ boy lay quietly on the first floor space to the right. (We don't have beds in our little hospital so patients lie directly on the hardwood floor.) His concerned father sat next to him. The father said that about ten days ago, the boy had developed a fever and right lower abdominal pain. He didn't want to eat anything but he had no vomiting or diarrhea. Then the boy's abdomen became hard. In fact, he did not want anyone to touch his belly. Over the next few days, however, he seemed to slowly improve.

"The father ended up bringing his son to our out-patient clinic a few hours before I would arrive. ██████, one of our senior staff members at ██████, checked him and felt the tender mass in his right lower abdomen. Although, the boy had no fever, and now described the pain as only coming and going, ██████ decided to admit him for further evaluation.

"I arrived later that day after a muddy, rainy exhausting walk over the mountain. Still suffering from the last vestiges of jetlag, I had pictured a nice slow start to my teaching rotation ... a little extra rest. Maybe I'd have to see a few diarrhea cases, a simple malaria patient, perhaps someone with a mild pneumonia. These are all common problems in the jungle but well within our usual scope of practice. I also hoped to take some uninterrupted time to learn about the brand new ultrasound machine I had carried with me from the US. It had been given by a very generous donor and included three different kinds of transducers, giving us the capability to evaluate a wide range of problems. I like to learn about new things.

"Unfortunately, an uncomfortable pattern in my life, seems to be the recurring need to learn some of those new things on the fly, often with a touch of desperation. After seeing the boy, I agreed with ██████ that he needed further evaluation. We unpacked the new ultrasound machine and attached the linear transducer. Although it took me a while as I fumbled around with the unfamiliar software, I could clearly see the abdominal mass on the new machine.

"Actually, I was shocked at how clear it was. Usually, our ultrasound images on the old machine's tiny DEET fogged screen looked like some hazy ghost clouds in a snow storm. I was never really sure what I was seeing. This clearly showed a mass that contained fluid and lay just beneath the abdominal muscles. Despite the visual clarity, I was still confused. From the patient's history, I was thinking he probably had an abscess from a ruptured appendix. And the ultrasound images seemed to confirm that. However, the boy now had no fever and although sore, didn't seem to be in that much pain. Freely admitting my lack of experience with this sort of thing, I sent the ultrasound picture out via e-mail (another new feature of the machine) to some very skilled colleagues and waited.

"As if the boy had deliberately waited to deteriorate until he could do so in our presence, overnight he developed a high fever and started having much more pain. As perverse as it may sound, this was actually an answer to prayer: "Lord, heal this boy or tell me what to do to help him." The fever and pain made it seem to me much more likely that it was indeed an intra abdominal abscess that would need surgically drained. Getting the boy to a general surgeon where he belonged, however, would mean carrying him in a stretcher for 2 days, enduring a long boat trip and would finish up by spending several hours in a bumpy car ride. That's a long ways of hard travel for someone with a ruptured appendix. I was torn. I really don't like to be in the position of having to do something to a patient that I have never done before. Even if the technical aspects of the procedure are easy, I have a pretty good imagination and can picture all sorts of things going wrong. I could see myself accidentally getting into the bowel. Hitting a major artery. I would give a large amount of money to get this kid to a more qualified doctor ... to someone who would find this sort of thing boring. In medicine, boring is good. But considering all the circumstances, I thought it would logically be better if we could drain the abscess at ███.

"I sent out a request to a few colleagues to walk me through a draining procedure using the ultrasound and we started IV antibiotics. Soon, technical advice came trickling in via e-mail. I asked a few colleagues who can sympathize with our situation, to pray for both patient and doctor. Slowly, hesitantly, like my little granddaughter's first attempts at walking ... I began to experience a confidence that the Great Physician himself was trying, admittedly with some difficulty, to help me help this boy.

"The next day we set up the "Operating Room". Armed with my active imagination, I pulled out every bit of technological back up we had ... just in case. We would use a very safe general anesthesia, ketamine. I still started the generator and hooked up the oxygen machine in case he stopped breathing. We readied the suction machine in case he aspirated. ████████, a trauma nurse with a no nonsense calming effect on all around her, set up the EKG monitor, meds, and got the patient ready. Mind you, although we were pulling out all of our stops, it was still nothing fancy. Our "OR" consisted of a rickety wooden table in a curtained off area of the hospital with Petzl headlamps for lighting. Ominously, one of the alarms on the monitor kept going off, sounding the "he's going to die" alarms in my subconscious. The boy lay on the table quietly watching us make all these preparations. A few minutes after giving the ketamine, his "watching" became a blank stare. And I began. I made the incision over the mass. Cauterized a few bleeders in the subcutaneous tissue by holding an old pair of forceps over an alcohol lamp from the lab. Probably not necessary, but it made me feel better pretending. I spread a pair of hemostats down through the muscle layers using the ultrasound images to guide me. And soon, just like that, we were looking at thick brown pus flowing from the wound. Ahh ... the joy of liberating the body of the burden of a festering abscess full of pus. It always seems so gratifying. I loosely sewed in a drain and we were done.

"The boy was pretty sore the next day but the fever was gone and the pain steadily improved. Once, I had a flare of my imaginative doctor doom alter ego, when I heard him crying. I was very relieved *to find out he was crying because he was hungry. (We were limiting his oral intake to liquids for a while.) Soon he was playing. I caught him smiling at a movie I took of him. After several days, we switched him to oral antibiotics. And tomorrow we are sending him home.*

*"For anyone in the surgical field, this is not a big deal at all. Probably boring. But for me it was well outside my comfort zone. Although I waited until I was sending the boy home to write this (in case he crashed and burned and God was actually trying to tell me something else ... oh ye of little faith applies to me for sure), I honestly felt God was orchestrating the whole thing. From the timing of the boy coming to the clinic, to actually having the new ultrasound machine with us when we arrived, to having all the medicine that we needed and to the timely input of our prayerful consultants, God was there."*[xi]

And this is my point, how many times do we miss God's provision for others just because it would call us out of our own comfort zone?

There are always two ways to look at an event. The father who is receiving the care that saved his son's life will view this as a miracle. My son the MD could have viewed it as a coincidence of the service he rendered, but without question he or God through him saved a little boy's life. The father of the boy will tell the story as a God given miracle. Be aware of what may look like a coincidence, but in reality it is a part of a miracle. Sometimes these God directed happenings occur over a long period of time, Sometimes the event occurs within a few seconds.

The second true story is also related to the concept of miracles and coincidence. A baby in a complicated delivery survived because things were in place waiting for the mother and the unborn child. The stretcher bearers were young and strong, and they carried her rapidly through the jungle in the rainy season to the (hospital's name withheld). My son was there at the little hospital. That was not a given. He could have been in the adjacent country. He could have been on his two day trip trying to get through the rain and the mud, and had not arrived yet. Here is his second story:

## **Strength and vulnerability**

*"Attracted by my headlight and the glow of this iPad screen, insects are crawling all over me in hoards. So I'll probably have to finish writing this in the morning ... for sanity's sake. But for tonight ... I think we just saved a life.*

*"I had finished lectures for the day when* ▓, *the medical director of the (Hospital's name withheld), came to tell me that we were expecting an emergency obstetrical case. He had gotten a message that one of our pregnant patients who had been seen earlier in the day for her prenatal check was on the other side of the hill with abdominal pain. I knew several pregnant women had come to the clinic that morning. But all the ones I knew about were only 30 to 32 weeks along ... way too early for labor pains to be beginning. Maybe it was something else? An abruption? Appendicitis?*

▓ *had already sent a team of several strong young men to carry the woman back. I waited for a half hour and as the team still hadn't returned, started walking in their direction. Maybe they were in trouble and needed help. More likely, I thought, there was no problem and they had stopped at Uncle Plaa's house for a wad of betal nut to chew and some* ▓ *stories. Nevertheless, on the way out, I grabbed 2 baby blankets and some exam gloves ... just in case. Even as I walked out of the hospital grounds, however, I was kicking myself ... my broken sandal would really be a problem if "just over the hill", instead turned out to be, "just in the next village" or "just over the next ridge". A common enough scenario. Furthermore, I had no flashlight and it was getting dark. All rookie mistakes and I knew better. Around here, worst case scenarios all too often become reality.*

"Thankfully, despite my paranoia, I met the team at the top of the hill coming down. The woman lay moaning in a hammock that was closely tied to a long bamboo pole ... the jungle ambulance. Two young ▬ men, sweaty, breathless and moving fast carried the precious bundle of mother and unborn child. Surrounded by verdant jungle and the roar of a nearby river, they were the picture of strength and vulnerability in a wild land. The rest of the spare carriers zoomed past, all practicality running. In fact, with my stupid sandal flopping like a flat tire, I couldn't keep up despite the fact they were carrying a person.

"Her clinic record had some problems. On today's earlier visit our patient had been labeled as being 32 weeks along in her pregnancy. And yet by her last menstrual period she was 39 weeks. At some point during her emergency return, her membranes had ruptured. As I examined her, the pain peaked and I noted her uterus becoming hard. She was definitely having contractions. Hard and fast. From the sound of her response, she was probably ready to start pushing. ▬, one of the young women our midwife is giving special attention to, would be this woman's medic. She gloved and did a vaginal check. I was doing a quick ultrasound to get position and maybe an estimation of the discrepant gestational age. ▬ looked at me and all she said was, "head" and showed about half a finger length left to go. The age of the baby was irrelevant for now. This little one was coming, ready or not. The baby's heart was good, and thus, without further ado, the second stage of labor began.

"After several pushes, however, I noted a small trickle of dark blood. "That's not good." A couple contractions later, I saw more blood. Then, the baby's head began to crown. I checked the baby's heart rate. 165. "Still OK". I continued to listen as the next contraction began. The baby's heart beat gradually slowed down. Way down. Until I lost it in the background of the mothers' pulse. This de-acceleration with the dark trickle of blood was most concerning. The placenta, the baby's only source of oxygen, was detaching. We were close to delivery. There was still hope. But that baby had to get out now. We urged mom to push hard.

"This was the woman's second baby and she knew how to push. In two more pushes, ▇▇▇ nicely controlled the delivery of the baby's head. The shoulders, body, baby girl parts ... and placenta! ... all immediately gushed out. This confirmed that our little patient probably had very little oxygen over the last several minutes of the delivery.

"And she looked it. Pale. No muscle tone. Not breathing. We dried, stimulated and suctioned. I asked ▇▇▇, our ER nurse to start breathing for the baby with an infant bag valve mask. The curious and usually talkative students peaking over the privacy curtain stood watching, unusually quiet.

"And then ... a pitifully weak squeak of a cry. She took a few breaths on her own. A few minutes more added a little pink to her color and some muscle tone. Then she was off and running. Demonstrating typical ▇▇▇ enthusiasm for a good meal she started nursing like her little life depended on it. I looked at her wrinkled, full term beautiful little foot. She was going to make it!

"Everything happened so fast, we really didn't have time to agonize over any decision. But I know very well how close we came to losing this little one. This could have gone so very wrong at several turns. In fact, I don't think she would survived if she had delivered at home, or the strong young ▇▇▇ men hadn't been so fleet of foot, or we didn't have the ability to do a simple resuscitation. Coincidence? Maybe. I have a friend who says he doesn't believe in coincidences ..."

## Side Note:

"One of the hardest decisions that we make at(Hospital's name withheld) is to decide who we send out to ▇▇▇ for a more definitive diagnosis or more advanced care. And who do we send *home to die. Taking patients through the ▇ tertiary medical system is expensive. And not just in monetary terms. Our patients speak (language) and sometimes (language). They don't speak (language). Technically, they are illegal immigrants and can be arrested on the spot. The (country) medical system graciously treats them anyway ... as long as someone pays their expenses. Furthermore, most of these patients do not have any experience with modern technology. Elevators, cars, flush toilets are unfamiliar. They need someone with them every step of the way. Taking a patient to modern facility for medical care involves much money and many man-hours. And that directly impacts what we have left over to work with at ▇▇▇▇ So we very carefully and prayerfully decide who we offer this service to and appreciate any help."[xii]*

From the perspective of the patients receiving the healing from this jungle hospital, the events were miracles. The father with his sick son and the woman in labor looked at potential death or loss of a loved one and there was healing through my son, the doctor. From the doctor's perspective it could be just a series of coincidental happenings. The new ultra-sound equipment just happened to be there. The doctor just happened to be there. God just happened to call the doctor when he was a very young boy to serve him in places with great need and where other doctors are reluctant to go. The doctor's presence was not a forgone conclusion. God put him there waiting to perform God's next miracle through the hands of a trained doctor. Going to a doctor is not a lack of faith. God gives all of us work to do. You do not pray for a miracle to cut your grass. You do what you can do. That is all of us. We take joy in knowing that our knowledge applied to people creates satisfaction and miracles. And when there is no hope, God shows up performing a miracle through his servants.

Christians usually have to be at the scene applying oil and praying to see miracles happen face to face with the person. That is our job. Jesus sent the seventy out with power. They came back rejoicing that the demons were subjected to them. Jesus corrected their misplaced joy. He remind them to get excited about having their names written down in the kingdom of Heaven.

Ananias had to go to Paul face to face. Philip had to go to the eunuch. Peter had to preach directly to the 3000 in their presence as recorded in Acts 2. Peter had to also go to Cornelius. Peter and John had to look directly in the eyes of the lame man at the temple's gate. There are many other Biblical examples of person to person ministry.

When prayer is offered up for a lost love one or someone is sick, in a distant place, what we are praying for usually is to have a Christian near by to go to that person and touch their life and provide the person's needs. God put the task of ministry in our hands. It is not a burden, but it is fun to work for God.

A remote healing or salvation can come directly from God when there is an elected person in God's cross-hairs. The original disciples and Paul are examples of God intervening directly without anyone else. These are the elected Christians. In addition to the elected, there are multitudes of the "whosoever will may come." In general, Christians are the hands and feet of God on this earth at this time. Of course God is God and He can do what he wants, so we will keep on praying for a remote healing or salvation of people at some far location.

There is value in praying for people listed in the church bulletin, but there are too many Christians that would never leave the sanctuary to go directly to the needy. The Bible is full of Christians facing the sick and the lost. The modern church is reluctant to do this. This is a requirement for each Christian to be willing to go.

My wife and I prayed a couple of times each day for my grandson who was an Army Ranger. "God save Luke in Afghanistan.", was our constant prayer. We were in Arkansas a world away. There was no way we could directly reach our grandson soldier. On his fourth deployment, the enemy planned an elaborate ambush. Four Rangers were killed and 23 were seriously wounded. One of the Rangers who died was Luke's best friend.

The dog handler turned his dog loose and the dog was blown up instead of my grandson. The dog saved his life. Luke was injured enough to get a Purple Heart, but his injury was minor compared to many of the other Rangers. Remote prayer works. Cards, letters, phone calls, and text messages can all help. But … We all need to say, "I will go. Send me." There comes a time when we get up off our knees and go into the thick of the battle. We are God's feet and mouth in many cases. Let us stop hiding in the sanctuary.

My life would have been much easier as a child if one Christian would have come to our house and told our family about the Lord Jesus Christ.

# CHAPTER 6: JUDAH

There are many readers that have their own miracles that they could write about. Some have been forgotten or went unrecognized. Some of these mysterious happenings were wrongly classified as coincidences, but the coincidences were actually longer term miracles. Some will be remembered forever with very grateful hearts what God did in their situation.

This next story is about Judah, my grandson. He was born to my fourth son and his wife, and Judah was their first baby. The baby was a beautiful baby of 9 pounds and he was going to be another red-head. I have three red-headed sons, and three red-headed grandsons.

Judah's grandmothers were both nurses, and they recognized that the baby was lethargic. Judah would not nurse. Judah was examined by doctors who made predictions of 2 days, 2 months, 2 years before he would die. Actually, I do not remember the precise prediction of his expected life except he was not supposed to survive very long. Today at 20 years old Judah is driving a car and has graduated from high school. He is now attending John Brown University and finished his first year successfully.

Again, Judah gets a pessimistic expectation of life from a recent visit to the doctor. The family was told to prepare for the end of life issues. Judah has a very bad heart and his arteries and veins from the lungs to the heart are spindly. I have asked his parents and Judah to write part of this chapter because it is a 20 year ride of depending on the Lord and praying for his healing. I personally expect his complete healing soon.

[I included a picture here of Judah after a near death experience on the operating table. My wife told me to take it out, which I obediently did to comply with her goal of toning the book down for a broader acceptance.]

Judah wrote the following for an English class at John Brown University. Here is his story unedited:

## My Early Life: [xiii]

"I'm here today only because of God. I could be dead now and according to the medical community I should be. God sometimes chooses to spare one life so that many others can be impacted and inspired for His glory! Why God chooses to allow some to die and spare others, I don't know, but it is all part of His plan in the end. God's provision is always the best. It may not seem the right thing at the time, but God will work all things for our good. If you open your eyes you just might see God's love and power, even in the most desperate of situations.

"My parents and I know God's timing all too well. I was born on July 7, 1995, in my parents house. My dad thought I was dead in his arms, but I wasn't. It was obvious that something wasn't right with me. My grandma, being a nurse, advised my parents that they should take me to the doctor. The doctors, right a way, knew that something was terribly wrong with me. The doctors started doing tests and found out that I had a heart problem. I was a very sick kid. I had my first heart surgery, at Arkansas Children's Hospital when I was thirteen days old. During that surgery they discovered that I had DiGeorge Syndrome. I had a second heart surgery a few days later. At three months of age I had a third surgery due to my inability to keep enough nutrition in my body. I was in and out of Arkansas Childrens Hospital the first couple years of my life. I almost died a few times, but through it all God was there. He showed up at just the right time and always had His way.

"Naturally with physical limitations like not being able to engage in physical activities because I get tired out easily, there are things I wish I could do. Unfortunately I can't. I would love to play some type *of sport or do something else that's physical. I've watched my siblings and others play sports all my life and rough house, but I've never been able to participate for long-term sessions because of my physical limitations. I've had many family members in the wars that America has fought since the Civil War and the Revolutionary War . I would follow in their footsteps if I had the physical ability to. If I had the chance I'd live in a healthy person's body for a day. I can't choose my genetics, but I don't dwell on what I can't do. My health has been good for several years. I haven't been admitted to the hospital since about 2007! I do get repeated infections every now and then, but besides that it hasn't been anything too severe. I instead focus on what I can do and let God use me that way.*

*"God has taught me many things over the years. I don't take my health for granted because of the many things that I've been through. I may be sick some days and be feeling better the next. I don't dwell on my health issues, but thank God for the life I have lived and health I have. I've learned to appreciate others for who they are and not wish that I could be healthy like they are and do everything that they can do. God has taught me about His faithfulness as well over the years. I wouldn't be here without God's faithfulness and His willingness to spare me so that my life can be used for His glory! He is faithful to finish what He has started!"*

*"Today thanks to God I'm a lot healthier now and haven't been admitted to the hospital for many years! I have done things that many doctors who knew me as a kid, wouldn't have thought I would do. I've lived abroad, graduated high school in Thailand, and I'm now a freshman in college! God's timing is the best. He might not provide your needs and wants when you want them, but his timing is always perfect."*[xiv]

I know of a number of people who rely totally on prayer and divine healing. If they would admit it, they think going to a doctor is a form of unbelief for them. If your grass needs mowing, you get the lawn mower out and mow it. If it is dinner time, you get the pots, pans, and food out and cook. If these folks have a tooth ache, some of them will go to a dentist. If they broke something where the bone is protruding through the skin, they will seek medical help. God allows people to learn skills and invent machines. Even in the Garden of Eden, God gave Adam and Eve work to tend the garden. When a doctor, through years of learning, has a knowledge of how to help the person's own body heal itself, he or she is happy to lessen the suffering and see healing take place. I have no guilt going to a doctor when I am sick or injured. In my not so humble opinion, medical skill should be used for the victim of the disease or injury. This gives doctors the opportunity at fixing the broken. The formula is simple:

Prayer First + Medical Help Second + Healing Prayer Last

With Judah, this formula or procedure was followed. The medical help ran out of options, and the family was left with looking to God to spare his life, which was miraculous and that is exactly what happened. Judah was supposed to die. Since the doctors and their knowledge couldn't do anything else, Judah and family looked exclusively to God. We saw how Judah lived and grew healthier. He is not totally repaired yet, but it is my firm belief that he will eventually be totally fixed. As that day approaches, I get more and more excited. This will be our time to dance into the temple leaping and dancing and praising God.

## CHAPTER 7: DAVID S

David S is a walking miracle. When I met him three years ago, he would accompany me calling. Calling is an activity evangelicals use to describe the pursuit of the lost sheep outside the church by knocking on doors in the evening to attempt to lead people to Christ. We are not the Jehovah Witness denomination, but we are just doing what the Bible said to do: "Feed my sheep."

At least we would invite them to church if the church is what it should be. It is not unusual to find an evangelical in a church who does not invite people to his or her church if the church is a Traditional church. The people will not stick there because first it is often very boring and second it is obviously filled with the elite of the community. I attend Grace-Point that started in a bar. People that I invite to church stick there. They come back. Some are homeless.

Mike Felder is the pastor and last Easter in this 2 year old fellowship at that time, there were 320 people in attendance with 16 baptisms in their horse tank they drag in for the occasion. Most of the people that I bring to Grace-Point stay. So evangelism consists of two parts. First is the guy in the street doing exactly what Jesus said to do in the Bible, and that is to find the lost sheep and introduce them to Jesus. Second is the church and their modus operandi to assist in maturing the new convert or in other words help make disciples.

When I was with David, we called on his people who were drug addicted felons that were either out of jail or headed to jail. I loved it because the folks were sick of their life style, and they wanted out.

David is a big guy. He about 6 feet 4 inches tall and over 260 pounds some time ago. He claims at that point in his life, two years ago, he was a baby fake Christian, whatever that means, and that is why he slipped and started using meth again. He disappeared from church and I knew he was in trouble. David was following the typical felon and a meth addict's performance.

His slide backwards happened when Gary C did not get healed of cancer. Larry R went with me one night to find an alcoholic who lived in an apartment complex where one house looks like another. We were at this address and we asked by name if this was where the drunk lived. The response was negative, but Larry R asked if anyone there needed prayer. Gary C said that he did because he was dying of cancer. That was the beginning of calls made to lead Gary to Christ and to heal him of terminal cancer . David went with me from that time forward. We lead Gary C to Jesus, and David baptized him. When Gary didn't get healed and died, David said to me, *"This calling and praying is pointless."* He stopped coming to church and he starting getting high again. David failed to realize at that point that Gary C was saved and with his Savior in heaven, which was a better solution to Gary's life than being healed. I saw David once in a filling station after his fall, and he was stoned and feeling no pain. After that I lost track of him completely.

Larry R was a chaplain at the Benton Country jail. Larry heard me talk about David. Larry and I met, and he told me David S was in jail. He was stealing to pay for his addiction, and he got caught. I started to write to David.

His prosecutor was tossing around the idea of a plea-bargain of 15 years in prison. The county was sick of him. He, of course, rejected this idea of 15 years.

During his 11 month incarceration, he started to draw pictures. At first he could not draw stick men, but his drawing skill improved. He wanted to draw a butterfly, but he could not because he could not visualize the details of a butterfly. While he was out in the recreation yard, a butterfly dropped down at his feet. This simple act somehow got David looking to God again. He prayed and read his Bible, and that was the beginning of David's miracle. He prayed that whatever happened to him, he would accept it as God's will. David knew that he would praise God from that point on.

One of the things that I did when David and I were working with Gary C was to take some pictures when David baptized Gary. These pictures were tools that would aid in David's release on probation. I sent the pictures to the public defender and she sent them on to the prosecutor. Getting religion in a foxhole or jail is not convincing to other people, but when they received a letter with a picture when David was out of jail, it was convincing. There was one other factor that David thinks was key. It was the fact that the prosecutor was getting married at the same time of David's trial. I am sure that added to the coincidences surrounding David's release from jail with probation. However, the prosecutor could of gotten a continuance or used an assistant. It all added to what David calls a "sweet deal". David went from a plea bargain of 15 years in prison to 6 years of probation. How cool is that?

I was still on Beaver Island in Michigan when David was released on August 19, 2013, which is my birthday. One of the problems that meth addicts have is they have burned all their bridges with family and friends who are sober. The only place left for them is back in other addicts' residences. This, of course, is the worst place to put those released from jail for drug use. David survived the short stay in his addict friend's house. I called Marshall O, a friend, and asked him to take care of David until I got back to Arkansas. Marshall interviewed David and decided to offer him a place to stay in a cabin in his back yard. Marshall is a farmer and had lots of needed repair work. He found that David was a highly skilled fabricator and welder. Marshall asked David if he ever thought about starting his own shop. David replied that he would like to do that. I got back from Michigan and knew that David could stay for a short time with Marshall and he needed transportation. Housing and transportation became our number one priority, and it was quickly supplied as I didn't think twice about how it would be done. God supplied the need, and we went to the next hurdle, which was a job.

I founded Ryan Engineering, and at 65 years-old I sold the business to my fourth son Dan, a mechanical engineer. When I was CEO, we built special machines for industrial clients. Dan followed a different plan doing structural design, and he formed a forensic group in Hot Springs, Arkansas. Ryan Engineering didn't use the machinery. Over time I bought back the equipment, and it made no sense at the time because we rarely used any of it. It was of course a divine plan waiting to happen.

With Marshall O suggesting to David that he should start a shop, and with me owning a complete shop of equipment, David had what he needed to open Shelton's Shop. This he did. He took calling cards and went to various industries telling about the shop and his story about his rededication to Jesus Christ. It wasn't long before he found work repairing trash dumpsters for the city. Shelton's Shop was in business.

[Go to www.actsoneeightinternational.com and click on the addiction button for David's own words about what happened. ]

David's wife was in prison. His son and daughter were not in the best situation. His son was on prescription pain medicine. His daughter asked him, "You are in jail and mom is in prison. Who do I call mom and dad?"

He took his son under his wing, and at that point in time he was drug free with a good job. If you work with the broken, backsliding into drugs is expected. Since each one of us after our conversion sinned, not quitting Jesus after the first sin is a rule of Grace. Eventually, when the Holy Spirit takes over, sin fades away. None of us in the evangelical business quit on a new convert after the first sin. With drug addiction, the sin has far reaching results with very broad recognition of the sin from other people. If we holy men see an attractive woman scantily dressed, we can sin, but our sin is within our hearts that we confess to God and ask for forgiveness in our prayer closet. Nobody knows, except God, that we just sinned. With the sin of addiction, everybody knows when the addict screws-up.

David's wife is now out of prison. David is the director of Haven House, which is a home for recovering drug addicts. He is involved in the leadership role of the Grace-Point church, and he is ministering to people living in Haven House who are off meth and are trying to follow Jesus.

A typical day for David is to take my call and listen to my story of finding where a fallen "gang banger" lives. This man had been in gangs in LA and was shot in the head losing an eye. David and I met his estranged wife at McDonald's. She gave me his address. Jose was temporarily living with his parent. David and I went to his parent's house. The parents are ready to run us off because they thought we were some of his drug buddies. As soon as they found out we were Christians doing what Christ said to do, their frowns changed to big smiles. We went inside and talked to their son. David starts talking and pacing back and forth. The words spilling out of his mouth were so profound that we both knew the Holy Spirit was speaking through him.

I took Jose over to talk to Pastor Mike. Shortly afterwards, David called me up and told me to go chill-out with our "gang banger". David said, "You put the worms on the hook and caught a fish. Now go clean him." I knew what he meant, and I interrupted my needed nap and "chilled –out". We had coffee together and talked about the future.

Even while this book was in the creation stage, Jose called me and needed $600 to reunite with his wife in another state. I called David and he interviewed Jose to see what the real story might be. We are very careful with donated money, and David's recommendation will make the decision as to whether Jose gets the $600 or not. We actually gave him half of what he needed.

David has written his story of his life without Jesus, and he is now writing his life's story with Jesus. He cannot change his past, but through Christ he can write an amazing story in the future. I have watched the miracle develop. He is not just conforming to a traditional Christian, but he is becoming the Holy Spirit filled individual that has changed his life and that of his whole family. He is also changing the life of many other young drug addicted felons.

It has been my privilege to watch an amazing miracle that is as impressive as raising the dead or healing the afflicted. Pray for David S------, that he remains strong in Christ, and that he isn't hurt by some unthinking Christian.

When a person is involved in this type of ministry, ask the question what if the person slips and falls. Good soldiers and sailors know what they will do if and when bad things happen. We need to know that the solution for the disappointment that comes when working with addicts who fail. It involves the old "F" word: Forgiveness! Keep on until the Holy Spirit tells you to quit.

# CHAPTER 8: THE BUSH

Moses had an encounter with God through a bush. The bush burned but was not consumed. Moses met God in a burning bush.

## *Exodus 3:1-10*

*1 "Now Moses kept the flock of Jethro his father in law , the priest of Midian: and he led the flock to the backside of the desert, and came to the mountain of God, even to Horeb. 2 And the angel of the LORD appeared unto him in a flame of fire out of the midst of a bush: and he looked , and, behold, the bush burned with fire, and the bush was not consumed . 3 And Moses said , I will now turn aside , and see this great sight, why the bush is not burnt . 4 And when the LORD saw that he turned aside to see , God called unto him out of the midst of the bush, and said , Moses, Moses. And he said , Here am I. 5 And he said , Draw not nigh hither: put off thy shoes from off thy feet, for the place whereon thou standest is holy ground. 6 Moreover he said , I am the God of thy father, the God of Abraham, the God of Isaac, and the God of Jacob. And Moses hid his face; for he was afraid to look upon God. 7 And the LORD said , I have surely seen the affliction of my people which are in Egypt, and have heard their cry by reason of their taskmasters ; for I know their sorrows; 8 And I am come down to deliver them out of the hand of the Egyptians, and to bring them up out of that land unto a good land and a large unto a land flowing with milk and honey; unto the place of the Canaanites, and the Hittites, and the Amorites, and the Perizzites, and the Hivites, and the Jebusites. 9 Now therefore, behold, the cry of the children of Israel is come unto me: and I have also seen the oppression wherewith the Egyptians oppress them. 10 Come now therefore, and I will send thee unto Pharaoh, that thou mayest bring forth my people the children of Israel out of Egypt.* (KJV)

A bush was used to convince me of the power of God in my

universe. To understand the details of this true story, two words are sufficient: I am a "snow bird". My wife and I live in Arkansas 6 months or more in the cold months, and 6 months or less on Beaver Island located 30 miles out in the middle of northern Lake Michigan. We have house sitters in Arkansas that take care of the lawn. When we came back from Beaver Island three years ago, one of our Azalea bushes was dead. There was not a leaf on the bush. The branches were dead and brittle. I looked at the bush as I entered our home. I wondered how I could remove the bush without disturbing the other bushes. I called my wife out to survey the loss. Both of us were a little saddened by the death of the Azalea bush.

We finished unloading our small cargo trailer. I walked by the bush one more time, and I heard a clear distinct voice that said, "Pray for the bush". What? I was alone on the sidewalk looking at the dead Azalea bush. The voice was spoken in rapid dialog. It was almost loud. I am certain that the voice was within my brain and not acoustical. I think if anyone was with me, they may not of heard the voice. I am not schizophrenic, but for a moment I wondered about it. Pray for a dead bush? I could not believe it. The bush was not that valuable. If it couldn't stand up to a hot Arkansas summer, let it die. What would it matter if I did pray for the bush? I looked up and down my street. There was no one to see what I thought was a crazy thing to do. I don't know when the idea crossed my mind that it was not about the bush, but it was a little practice session where I could learn to hear and respond to the voice of God. After looking around to see that nobody was watching, I bowed my head and prayed for God to heal this dead Azalea bush. I went inside and called to my wife to come and look closely at the dead bush. She came out, and as I remember we broke off a few leafless and brittle branches. I told her the story of the voice that wanted me to pray for the bush. I don't recall what she said or her reaction. She probably thought about her marriage vow of "for better or worse". I did not water or fertilize the bush. I went into the house and started putting things away from our months on Beaver Island.

The next morning I went out to look at the bush. There were little green sprouts starting to form. Sue came out to look at the bush. We just looked at each other and wondered what in the world was going on? Every morning we came out to a bush that was coming back to life. I could not see any sense in this miracle. I have a disabled grandson for whom I have offered many prayers. His story is in the previous chapter. Even though he has completely passed all the medical predictions, he still needs oxygen because his weak heart is not strong enough to supply his body requirements. Heal Judah and let the bush die. So I looked for a deeper meaning and teaching. Jesus said that it was expedient that he go away so the Holy Spirit could come and teach us.

***John 14:26 But the Comforter, which is the Holy Ghost, whom the father will send in my name, he shall teach you all things, and bring all things to your remembrance, whatever I have said to you.***

I believe that the bush was a teaching time for me. When God wants a miracle, it will be performed. I needed to be reassured that miracles are still happening, and God still speaks to people directly. The bush was a simple object lesson for me.

One of the theological discussions that is covered in the next chapter is why, in the Lord's prayer, we are instructed to pray, "thy will be done on earth as it is in heaven". If God suspends free will and is in control of everything on earth why is everything such a mess and why does the Lord's prayer instruct us to pray that God's will be done on earth as it is in heaven?

# CHAPTER 9: TRUTH FROM THE WORD

I have a PHD in engineering from Michigan State University. I have always been an engineer in my adult life. I do not know Hebrew and my one course in Greek from a seminary has long since been forgotten, and a high school course in Latin has also been totally forgotten. I cannot base my theories on the translating the original language, but my ability to read and logically analyze is in very good order. I have done this in working for manufacturers with design problems, and more recently with lawyers in civil cases involving law suits for defectively designed products where finding evidence was important.

All the various translations of the Bible are very similar, which means the ancient texts have been translated properly. My writing is based on these translations, and unless the Bible, as I know it, is terribly flawed, my interpretation of the truth is valid.

I hear many writers, theologians, pastors, and Christian say, "God is in charge". He could be if He would suspend free will to control what happens on the earth. Let us assume that God is in charge of the events on earth. Looking at all the wars, the Nazi reign, murders, pedophiles, and victims in general, God could be accused of not doing a very good job of being in charge. The Lord's prayer should settle the issue. Why would Jesus encourage Christians to pray , "thy will be done on earth as it is in heaven." It is clearly a prayer to have God's will done on earth as it is in heaven. Apparently, His will is not necessarily done on earth, but it is desired and Jesus taught us to keep this in our prayers.

When we pray for His will to be accomplished on earth in a free will manner, God can direct his Holy Spirit filled followers to follow what they are directed to do and where they are to go. Therein God is presenting his plan for the Spirit filled person's life. Our problem is hearing and seeing what we should be doing to carry out His will on earth. If we see, hear, know what we are to do, we may still disobey either wantonly or unsure of the message as to whether we are interpreting things correctly. Due to the free will of men and women, God's will may or may not be carried out on earth.

God has, in my own life, moved the proverbial chess pieces around to help me follow his plan for my life. God wants his will to be done on earth as it is in heaven. He does his part, but we have to follow the Holy Spirit's directed path. Free will reigns, both good and evil. For the chosen, He lightly intercedes with what we think are coincidences, a wee small voice, or pertinent truth from the Bible.

Even though we pray "thy will be done on earth as it is in heaven", we know that free will is always an option. We want the best for ourselves and others. God has a plan for our life, but often we do not follow that plan. Sometimes it is deliberate. Sometimes it is because we didn't listen or could not understand what we were supposed to do. For some Traditionalists, they are following a false concept that has nothing to with what God says or wants. Whatever, the perfect plan is not implemented. I can look back and see that either I was very lucky or God, for some reason, moved my chess pieces around and I followed. Maybe He felt sorry for all my suffering as a child. I don't know what happened, but I rejoice in my soul mate. We both realize that something miraculous happened to us.

It is imperative that we take our decisions seriously. They make the difference. Pray about everything. A friend of mine gets into his closet with the door shut. He prays that his mind is emptied of his ideas, and that any thoughts in the prayer closet are coming from the Holy Spirit.

Sometimes God calls us out of a successful situation into something that we might not choose. Philip is a great example. Most of us would have stayed in the city of Samaria because God was moving, and good things were happening.

*Acts 8: 6-8:* *"Then Philip went down to the city of Samaria, and preached Christ unto them. 6 And the people with one accord gave heed unto those things which Philip spake , hearing and seeing the miracles which he did . 7 For unclean spirits, crying with loud voice, came out of many that were possessed with them: and many taken with palsies , and that were lame, were healed."*

**Then God sent Philip to go south on the desert road:**

*Acts 8:26-31: 26 And the angel of the Lord spake unto Philip, saying , Arise , and go toward the south unto the way that goeth down from Jerusalem unto Gaza, which is desert. 27 And he arose and went : and, behold , a man of Ethiopia, an eunuch of great authority under Candace queen of the Ethiopians, who had the charge of all her treasure, and had come to Jerusalem for to worship , 28 Was returning , and sitting in his chariot read Esaias the prophet. 29 Then the Spirit said unto Philip, Go near , and join thyself to this chariot. 30 And Philip ran thither to him, and heard him read the prophet Esaias, and said , Understandest thou what thou readest ? 31 And he said , How can I , except some man should guide me? And he desired Philip that he would come up and sit with him."*

Philip was called out of a revival to minister to one man. People were being healed and saved. Yet God wanted the eunuch specifically, and he sent Philip. It was no coincidence that Philip was sent to the desert by God to minister to the eunuch. The outcome was up to Philip and the eunuch. Free will ruled the scene even though God manipulated the players in this real life drama.

*John 14:12 "Verily, verily, I say unto you, He that believeth on me, the works that I do shall he do also; and greater works than these shall he do; because I go unto my Father."*

John 14:12 is a very interesting scripture. This is pretty plain stuff. The works that Jesus did, which included miracles, his followers will also do. To make this fit many Traditionalist views, the scripture would have to read: "You Disciples will do greater works than these, but keep in mind that all the works, miracles included, will end with your death." He did not say that. History will bare it out that miracles have continued and great ministries have happened.

Jack Deere, a one time supporter of this idea that miracles and healing stopped, changed his thinking when he could not prove this concept from the scriptures. Jack Deere was faculty at Dallas Theological Seminary. The reader should go on line and read what this seminary teaches.

The most recent miracle that I have observed is related to my own health. At 80 years old, I am in good health except I have had atrial fibrillation, which is an irregular heart beat. My heart would go for about two or three pumps and then produce a sound like some drunken drummer on the snare drum. This was something that I would live with for the rest of my life by taking a blood thinner so blood clots would not form. My atrial fibrillation had become a permanent condition. I expected to live with this problem until it killed me or caused a stroke.

Larry and Julie R and my wife wanted to pray for me. Never turn down prayer. Since it was not a high priority on my concern scale, but it should have been, I agreed as I sat back in my comfortable chair with three peoples' hands on my head and chest and listened to their prayers. I don't remember when I noticed my heart was beating out a steady beat, but it did. After a period of time, I went to my trusted doctor. "Is the beat steady?" I asked. Doctor B listened and agreed that, at that moment, the beat was normal. At a later appointment, he did an EKG. It was normal. Then he put me on a 24 hour monitor. The Atrial Fibrillation was gone. Praise God! Another miracle is witnessed, and Atrial Fib bites the dust!

# CHAPTER 10 FINDING SUE

When it comes to women, men think there are lots of fish in the ocean, and when one relationship fails there will be another with someone else. Women can think the same. However, I found my soul mate through an unbelievable set of circumstances that turned out to be the best overall miracle. I think it is worth telling how I met my wife.

After my first serious girl friend led me to my Savior, God's plan continued working. Mary E. was studying for her master's degree at Western Michigan University. When she went to summer school, she wanted me to join her at WMU. I did join her for the summer classes. When she went home to her teaching job, I stayed for two more semesters.

During the fall and winter semester, Mary E. and I broke up. I started dating other girls. I met a girl in Calculus that caught my eye. I asked her out, and we double dated. There was something there between us, but she had a number one choice and I was number two. I got tired of being on her second team and I dated one of her friends. The friend turned out to be very interesting. She could drink everybody under the table. She had more off the wall ideas than anyone I had ever known. She asked me if I would take her home at the end of spring semester. I agreed. This was an important step in finding Sue, my true soul mate.

I asked my best friend Jack if he would meet me in Monroe, Michigan where I would drop the current girl friend at her home, and then we could go to Detroit and look for a job. Jack agreed to the plan.

Before our rendezvous to go job hunting, I stayed in Monroe and dated the latest prospect. I will call her Miss VS. Miss VS wanted to go to a wedding reception. She lectured me before we arrived at the reception. She was going to dance with whomever asked, and I was not to get jealous. She claimed to have many friends, and friends were important to her. I later found out that the people she called friends barely knew her. Anyway, at the dance, I danced with every girl I could find. Miss VS and I did not dance a single dance. Every time I looked for her she was standing on the side. No one asked her to dance. This humiliated her. She was upset at me from that point on and she and I were history, which may have been a very good coincidence.

About that time, Jack and I met in Monroe to go to Detroit, I had no girlfriend and very little money. We combined job hunting with beer drinking, and both of us were running rapidly out of cash. Finally with no success finding work, Jack and I went south to Toledo where he got on the toll road and went home to Mongo, Indiana. For some crazy decision on my part, I stayed in Toledo, which was another step closer to Sue. That night I slept under my old Chevy in a rain storm within sight of the toll-road. I had very little money in my pocket, but I did have the diamond ring that I got back from Mary E when we parted. I also had an alto saxophone that was one of the three reasons this woman and I parted company. I would have played anywhere I could get a gig. I love music, and I love playing in a band. Mary E. would not even consider me playing in a band in a beer joint. That old saxophone did me a favor in finding Sue.

The next morning I headed to a pawn shop where I hocked my sax and the ring. I then went to Al Sautter's employment agency and listed my service as a draftsman. That night I stayed in a wino hotel with the bath down the hall and empty wine bottles in the closet. The sheets were clean, and it was still raining outside. The next day I got an interview with Dana Corporation. They wanted a draftsman, and they hired me. This was a big step toward my future soul mate Susan.

I landed the job and got an apartment with a shared bath down the hall. Again it was a dump, but I advanced from the wino hotel to a hillbilly apartment. There was little improvement in the shared bathroom. [My proof reader suggested I take out the part about the people who didn't understand indoor plumbing.] There was a gas grill in the apartment, and I cooked myself food poisoning over the weekend. I thought I was going to die. I wrote a goodbye note to whomever found my body where I stated that I did not kill myself. This was another step toward Sue.

After recovering from the food poisoning, I moved almost immediately to the YMCA. I never learned to cook and I thought a sleeping room and a greasy spoon restaurant were in order. In the meantime, friends at Dana Corporation felt sorry for me and fixed me up with a double date. For some crazy reason, I took my mandolin with me to show off to this new girl. I played and sang some of my songs in the backseat. I asked her out the next night, which was a weekend night. She agreed only because she could not figure out a way out of dating the mandolin man again.

So I got ready for this big date. I was headed out the door to a restaurant across the street when I heard my name called out over the PA system. I walked back to the counter where I was directed to a phone on the wall. "Hello." She started in with a series of excuses. Her Grandmother died, and she had a very sore throat, and there were other excuses. The girl was gutless. She could have told me she hated dating the mandolin man. Anyway, I got the message, and slammed the phone down and headed out again to the greasy spoon restaurant. Just before I walked out the door, I turned and looked down this long hall. I saw a mysterious blue light coming out of a door near the end of the hall. I decided to check it out. When I am angry, I tend to walk fast. I was doing 3 to 4 miles per hour when I turned right into this large room where I thought that the blue light originated.

I didn't see any blue lights, but to my left there was a stage and on the stage there was a band. Due to my fast walking, I was a good distance from the door when the band struck the first notes of the next dance. I was looking to my left, but when I turned around, there she was standing right before me. She had on a green plaid skirt with a white blouse and a vest. I didn't know what to do except ask her to dance because I was out on a dance floor too far from the door to escape. She said yes to my dance request. "What's your name?" She replied that her name was Sue Double. "What do mean Sue twice like Sue Sue?" She informed me that her last name was Double.

We danced and danced. Finally I asked her to the coffee shop down the street near the YMCA. We sat at the counter looking in the mirror at each other, and telling our stories. I should say I was probably telling my story. Sue tends to be very quiet.

I asked her out on a date the next night. She told me she was going home to her parents' house, but she would go if I picked her up at her parents' house. She gave me the address and how to reach her home. What I didn't realize was that this girl could not give directions and couldn't find her way around very well. I went from downtown on the Anthony Wayne Trail to Western Avenue. I was to turn left and drive until I found her street. I had the house number. I followed her directions and ended up at a dead end in the Maumee River. I began to believe this is number three girl that has dumped me. Miss VS from Monroe told me I would make her unhappy because I danced with other women and she did not get to dance at all. Maybe it was just a free ride to Monroe, Michigan, but she dumped me rather directly. The second woman didn't like my mandolin playing and gave me excuses, which were lies. The third one just gave me bad directions. I was sure that I had been dumped three times in a row.

I turned around, and at the Anthony Wayne Trail there was an ice cream store on the corner. I decided to go in and ask if anyone knew where Sue's address was. I went into the store, and asked where Durango Drive was located. Everybody in the store thought there was no Durango Drive in Toledo. I turned, and I picked up my pace and headed back to my car. I was headed home. Stood up again.

However a middle aged woman jogged out toward me telling me to wait. She said she thought there was a Durango Drive the other way. I should have turned right, but I was directed by Sue to turn left. This was a very big step toward meeting my soul mate. I almost abandoned the date. When I got to her house she was there with her family waiting to go out on our date. If I would have realized this was my soul mate and knew of our future together, I would have fallen down on her front room rug and worshiped her. But at the time I didn't know what happiness would come out of a union with this woman.

Even though I was a 4-H club member where I raised hogs to show and I was keenly aware of the importance of the genetics of the male and female pigs, I must confess that I related that to human beings back then. Unscientifically, I have seen enough to develop my theory that when stupid marries stupid the children have the potential to inherit the not so smart genes. Stupid is sometimes defined as being unable to get good grades in school. But there is more to the story than grades in high school. Since school fails to measure creativity, personality, courage and drive, there are many school-book limited people who succeed because these other assets are more important to success than reading a book and understanding or remembering what the textbook was trying to explain. Poor grades in school often have such a negative affect on the student that the person assigns themselves to the "loser" category. However, good grades will be great assets for people with creativity, personality, courage and drive. (I must be careful here because Sue will read this.) Sue had the genetic quality to give birth and pass on her qualities to my five sons . My five sons are book smart, creative, courageous and have drive. I left out personality because I had a role in their conception. Sue's parents were at the top of their classes scholastically. My mother was a scholar and my father was creative. Dad dropped out of high school before graduating. He was creative, courageous and had a very good personality. He lacked drive, but not to a fault after he became a

Christian.

Remember that the two top generals in the Second World War, Eisenhower and Marshall, were at the bottom of their graduating class from college. Eisenhower became president and Marshall ran the military.

My goal is to simply point out factors involved in procreation. In my farmer 4-H mind, Sue had what it takes to be the perfect mother. She was the perfect mother and wife. She would come into the house and if there was a son or later a grandbaby playing on the floor, she immediately got down on the floor with the child. Everybody remarks what a wonderful person she is. Then they look at me and wondered how the poor girl ended up with me. At least she thinks I am the greatest!

# CHAPTER 11 THE GREATEST MIRACALES

This book is written so that the readers will look back at his or her life and remember the miracles. This will increase faith. Eliminating suffering is important, and we will sing and dance for the healing of the flesh. However, the biggest miracle in my life was when Jesus saved me, and then came to live inside me. It got even bigger when my entire family was saved.

***Colossians 1:27 "Christ in you, the hope of glory."*** )KJV) It is important to understand that the Bible is not talking about something happening outside people, but it is something happening within.

***John 14:17 "Even the Spirit of truth, whom the world cannot receive, because it seeth him not, neither knoweth him, but ye know him, for he dwelleth with you, and shall be in you."*** (KJV)

When Jesus was baptized by John the Baptist, this was and is much more than a Bible story. This is what happened. ***John 1:32-33 "And John bare record saying, I saw the Spirit descending from heaven like a dove, and it abode upon him. And I knew him not: but he that sent me to baptize with water, the same said unto me, Upon whom thou shalt see the Spirit descending and remaining on him, the same is he which baptizeth with the Holy Ghost."*** (KJV)

***Matthew 3:16-17 "And Jesus, when he was baptized, went up straightway out of the water, lo, the heavens were opened unto him, and he saw the Spirit of God descending like a dove, and lighting upon him. And lo a voice from heaven saying, This is my beloved Son, in whom I am well pleased." Then Jesus went to the desert where he fasted 40 days and was tempted by the Devil, then to His ministry, and finally to the Cross.*** (KJV)

"What If" there is more power possible for a believer? "What If", instead of acting like a weak, non-witnessing, pew warming Pharisee there was more. "What If" there was a resemblance of Christ in His followers. Grace means unmerited love, and that was played out by Jesus on the cross. It does not mean to keep on sinning. The sin riddled person who never witnesses, who spends one hour per week in a pew, who rarely reads the words of Jesus out of the Bible, and who actually looks a lot like the world is missing something, and maybe that missing link is the Holy Spirit. What does the Bible say about the possibility of believing but not receiving?

**Acts 19:1-7 And it came to pass that while Apollos was at Corinth, Paul having passed through the upper coasts came to Ephesus: and finding certain disciples, He said to them, Have ye received the Holy Ghost since ye believed? And they said unto him, We have not so much as heard whether there be any Holy Ghost. And he said unto them, Unto what then were ye baptized? And they said, Unto John's baptism. Then said Paul, John verily baptized with the baptism of repentance, saying unto the people that they should believe on him which should come after him, that is, on Christ Jesus. When they heard this, they were baptized in the name of Lord Jesus. And when Paul had laid his hands upon them, the Holy Ghost came on them, and they spake with tongues and prophesied. And all the men were about twelve." KJV)**

I remembered my own history. At the Lima EUB church near Howe, Indiana in the winter of 1956, I had my first encounter with the reality of Christ being alive and working in this world. I was converted from being an atheist to a believer then and there, due to the fact that I saw a vision of an angel in brown peasant garb staring at me. I was emotionally shaken, and I not only asked God to forgive me of my sins but I believed I was a Christian. Sometime later my girlfriend asked me to call on a certain person that I remotely knew and tell him about my experience at the altar. My response was "no way." I was not about to "call" on a sinner and tell them about Jesus. I could not and I would not do it, much to the disappointment of my Mary E. The Holy Spirit had not yet taken control of me.

I started to read the Bible. I did not have a Traditionalist teaching me what the Bible said. I could read, and I could understand what I read on my own. I read about tongues, healing, and prophesying. I assumed the Bible was true. I was shocked to find out that some Traditionalist have a neat way to leap over scriptures that are not part of their dogma. I don't want to emphasize tongues, but it was very plain that after 1 Corinthians 13 there came 1 Corinthians 14.

***1 Corinthians 14: 5 "I would that ye all spake with tongues, but rather that ye prophesied for greater is he that prophesieth than he that speaketh with tongues, except he interpret, that the church may receive edifying".*** (KJV)

***1 Corinthians 14:18 "I thank God , I speak with tongues more than ye all."***(KJV)

How plain are the scriptures. How plain is the scripture the Traditionalists cling to with their interpretation of the following:

***1 Corinthians 13:8-12 "Charity never faileth: but whether there be prophecies, they shall fail; whether there be tongues, they shall cease, whether there be knowledge, it shall vanish away. For we know in part and we prophesy in part. But when that which is perfect is come, then that which is in part shall be done away. When I was a child, I spake as a child, I understood as a child, I thought as a child; but when I became a man, I put away childish things. For now we see through a glass darkly; but then face to face: now I know in part, but then shall I know even as also I am known."*** (KJV)

***"For now we see through a glass darkly, but then face to face: now I know in part, but then shall I know even as I am known."*** KJV) The interpretation of this, if there were no agenda, is that all the gifts of the Holy Spirit will not be needed when we are face to face with Jesus in glorious heaven. We will be face to face with our Savior. Everything that we did on earth stops because we are face to face with our Redeemer. It is strange language to say face to face with the Bible.

***"But when that which is perfect is come, then that which is in part shall be done away."*** Paul is not talking about the Bible, which did not exist at the time. He is clearly talking about being face to face with our Lord. This is the weak argument by some Traditionalists that fail to believe in the power and purpose of the Holy Spirit. This Holy Ghost power is needed more today than ever.

In modern times, Christians are attacked and killed overseas. Christians are being thought to be fools by the liberal media in the USA. Muslims kill anyone that does not belong to their version of Islam. Christians are the Muslims' enemy. Christians are supposed to love and pray for their enemies. It is hard to understand why Christians are persecuted with the beliefs held by the majority. If a Christian lives next door, there will be no coveting of your stuff, no lusting after your wife or husband, only the truth will be uttered by the Christian, and he or she will love you , help you, and pray for you. Why would anyone be against Christian neighbors? When people become Christians, they become ideal citizens. This hatred of Christians makes no logical sense except in the contents of what Paul said in ***Ephesians 6:12 "For we wrestle not against flesh and blood, but against principalities, against powers, against the rulers of the darkness of this world, against spiritual wickedness in high places."*** (KJV)

The Christian haters are robotic people controlled by the demonic. As a non-Christian, you can theoretically slap the holy people, and they are taught to turn the other cheek. If they don't, at least they will feel bad for not following the teaching of Jesus and punch back.

Real Christians love homosexuals, but according to the Bible it is defined as a sin.

***Romans 1:26 "For this cause God gave them up unto vile***

*affections; for even their women did change the natural use into that which is against nature,"*(KJV)

*Romans 1:27 "And likewise also the men, leaving the natural use of the woman, burned in their lust one toward another; men with men working that which is unseemly, and receiving in themselves that recompense of their error which was meet."* (KJV)

*1 Corinthians 6:9 "Know ye not that the unrighteous shall not inherit the kingdom of God? Be not deceived; neither fornicators, nor idolaters, nor adulterers, nor effeminate, nor abusers of themselves with mankind,* (KJV)

*1 Corinthians 7:2 "Nevertheless, to avoid fornication, let every man have his own wife, and let every woman have her own husband."* (KJV)

The last thing that an evangelist wants to see is sin, which does not hurt others, to be legislatively controlled or controlled by society or by pressure from religious people. My personal view is to encourage sinners to sin if they are so inclined. After sin has taken its toll on the sinners, they are great candidates for salvation. The converted hard core sinners are also great evangelists once they are saved. Rarely will the person who found Christ at an early age and never smoked, drank, did drugs, or committed fornication have a clue about how miserable a good sinner is. These folks tend to not want to offend anyone by confronting them with the Gospel. The hard sinner assumes everybody lost is in the depth of sin that he or she was. The sheep finders have compassion and courage to face the demons of hell out there in the world.

In defense of the pure at heart person raised in the church, I wish that I had been like that, but with a knowledge of the hurt caused by sin. Before we take anyone into our ministry in Haven House, the question is asked: "Are you sick of your life?" If they say yes, then there is hope. That sickness of life comes from hard core sinning.

Haven House is a home for people addicted to drugs and alcohol who are sick of their life style. [Again, go to www.actsoneeightinternational.com for details.]

So the reader does not think that the author's thinking is off base, let us look at what Jesus said:

**Revelations 3:16 "So, then because you are lukewarm and neither hot nor cold—I will spue thee out of my mouth."** (KJV)

When someone truly becomes a new creature in Christ, this exceeds the signs, wonders, healing, prophesy, and other marvels. Conversion is a miracle that lasts the life time of the believer, and it creates a ticket to heaven where the convert will never die. How great is that? People change.

If the evangelist is active, there will be encounters that are positive where the sinner is powerfully converted. There will also be a number of people who will pray the right prayers, and say the right words, but nothing happens. There is no conversion. Sometimes, this procedure is done over and over with no real results. The evangelist witnesses to the lost sheep tells them what Christ can do. This is done with words from the Holy Spirit and the Word of God. His Word will not come back void. But there is an idea floating around that you do not have to say anything. All you have to do is to live a good life before the sinner, and finally the sinner will be so impressed with your life style that he or she will ask the Christian why he or she is so wonderful. Then, and only then, will the chicken evangelist open his or her mouth and speak about the Lord. What a lie that is. When I met the goodie silent Christians before I was saved, I thought there was something wrong with them, and not me. They didn't drink, dance, cuss or chase women. The Christians were, in my sinful life's opinion, a bunch of boring people, and I certainly wanted nothing to do with them. If this stupid theory really worked, Paul and all the people of the New Testament could have simply shown the folks their nice personalities and there would have been no persecution. If someone wants to see me sin, tell me that all you have to do is be an excellent example and the world will become Christian. Of course the evangelist has to be an excellent example, but it takes a Christian to present the Word to sinners knowing that this action will not return unto them void. I hope I puke in the presence of people who tell me that being good is the key to evangelism.

However, when the witness opens his or her mouth, powerful words come out and penetrate the mind of the sinner. The Holy Spirit is there, and the sinner comes under conviction. The Christian witness leads this person to the Lord. Yet the witness must be an outstanding example of devoted love for Jesus. Witnessing, as was accomplished in the New Testament, has the potential of rejection, persecution, and stress. Hopefully, there are people who are courageous enough to do what must be done to have Jesus save the masses.

When Reverend C came to my Dad and Mother's house he didn't do the usual small talk about weather, jobs and family. He simply pointed a long finger at my 55 year old Dad and said "Leonard you need Jesus." My alcoholic father broke down and cried over his sins. Dad, Mom, and my youngest sister got down on their knees with the couch as an altar, and they poured out their hearts to God. They all were soundly converted. I was out of the home on my own. For years I asked why someone did not come when we were children and save us from the abuse that was prevalent in an alcoholic's home.

A few stories of the author's witnessing should prove that the direct in your face approach to evangelism works. Building relationships is important, but it is not completely essential. It is sort of like being good in the presence of the lost. God's Word works without long term relationships. The Gideon Bible in a drawer in a hotel has been the instrument of conversion to Christianity. Witnessing is the Bible on two feet walking and talking.

Ed B was an alcoholic headed toward a divorce from his second wife in Kalamazoo, Michigan. He and his wife lived in poverty, and he walked on thread bare carpets in a small house. He and Mary didn't have any children in their marriage. Harold W, my pastor, sent me and Clarence M over to Ed B's house.

Clarence M was a successful business man who was into real estate development. The target, Ed B, may have been unemployed at the time. We knocked on Ed's door and got into the home. Of course we shared Christ and told Ed and Mary about the miracles and the love of Jesus Christ. Usually, we have to explain why there is so much pain in this wicked world. Someone may have told them that God has a plan in their life and is in charge. There is a plan, but following the plan may or may not materialize. It happened too long ago to remember the details of our conversation. Perhaps Ed couldn't understand why his father was lost at sea in WWII if God were in charge. If God is in charge of the earth why are things so evil? Wars, rapes, and murders can be the topics of a typical newscast.

The evangelist must have an answer for the typical questions. "If God's in charge, He is not doing a very good job of being the boss of the earth." We would have explained that God is not in charge. This is a world with people who have the God given right of free will. We can do anything we want to do. The act may have consequences, but we have the right to do whatever pleases us. Then we may have explained things with the Lord's prayer: **"Thy will be done on earth as it is in heaven."** A person does not pray for the will of God to be done if it is already being done. That's the answer.

Clarence and I were not getting too far with this cold turkey call so we told Ed and Mary that we would be back the coming Thursday to hold a Bible study. I normally do not force a Bible study on people, but the Spirit of the living God made the Bible study happen. We came every Thursday night for a Bible study. Mary and Ed invited friends and a dish to pass, which created a Bible study with a meal. This went on for a few weeks. One Wednesday night I got a call from

Ed. His words were slurred, and he was obviously inebriated. I was at my dinner table with guests. I motioned for the family and friends to be quiet. Ed continued to tell his story. He said that he just saw Jesus. He asked, "Would I pray for him"? So I begin to pray for drunken Ed B. Jesus revealed himself to Ed that Wednesday night while he was intoxicated, and Ed became a Christian. He came to church every time the doors were open after his conversion, and he gave his testimony the first Sunday after his encounter with the Lord. Mary followed her husband into the Christian fold. Ed went to work for Clarence M and started making big money. His marriage was saved, and his financial situation improved to the point that Ed was financially comfortable. Ed told me later that he got drunk every Wednesday night so he could stand the Bible study on Thursday. Ed and Mary became friends. Years later I visited Ed. I asked him if he was calling on the lost on Thursdays. He said he was calling on the sinners Tuesdays and Thursdays. What we didn't know was that besides leading Ed and Mary to Christ, Clarence and I had taught Ed how to evangelize people. Ed soon left his mentors behind as he became a powerful witness for our Lord.

Gary S was 16 years old and lived back a lane in Oklahoma with his mother, father, and sister in a trailer home. His mother, Patsy, came to church and put a check mark on the visitor's card that indicated she wanted to be a Christian. I wanted to call on her and lead her to Jesus. The only calling partner that I could get was a man recovering from a stroke. He walked with a cane, and was willing to go out calling so he could improve his speech. He was an old man and was a bit peculiar. He was harmless, but he collected high school girls pictures, and he carried them in his pocket in a plastic holder that would fold up picture size but would unfold like an accordion. The unrolled pictures were at least three feet long. The pictures came into play when we got inside the home.

To find Patsy S, I had to go to the rural post office and find out where she lived. My old friend with the cane and pictures was with me that night we found the lane leading back to the house trailer.

The gate was closed and there was a sign that said something like "Surviving Trespassers will be shot again". I opened the gate, drove in, and got back out to shut the gate. Every cowboy knows that this is the task of the passenger, but my friend, recovering from a stroke, was not up to the task. It was dark, and the lane had deep ruts so that the bottom of my car dragged on the hump in the middle. After a time of driving, we could see the lights of the trailer. It sat on a hill beside one large tree. Concrete blocks were used as steps up and into the sliding glass door of the trailer. Also there were a number of dogs circling and barking ferociously. My partner couldn't run so I had the advantage. The next obstacle was to get the old man, who was recovering from a stroke, up into the trailer. We got to the next hurdle, which were the steps. The dogs were still deciding if they had the courage to attack. I helped my partner up into the trailer, and finally we were inside without being attacked by the dogs. The family was all there. Steve the father was drunk sitting in a recliner with what we assumed was a loaded shotgun within reach.

My old friend immediately pulled out the pictures of the high school girls and started showing them to the family. I told him to put his pictures away because we were there for some other reason than to show this family what he called his girls. He obeyed, and I got down to business. My calling partner was not much of an asset to the task at hand, but when God is in something, the comedy team of Laurel and Hardy could have accomplished the task.

My main focus was on Patsy who had put on her visitor's card at the church that she wanted to become a Christian. Steve was drunk, and I had some experience with alcoholics so I was also focused on him. I would deal with the kids, but they were a side issue in this case. This would turn out differently. Gary S was 16 and his sister a bit younger. Actually, we didn't know at the time, but Gary was receiving much more from our visit that we ever expected.

I started my case for Christ by telling them how I walked into church an atheist, saw a vision of an angel, and was saved. I may have read the Roman's Road. I don't remember the details, but Patsy prayed first and became a Christian. She was solid in her repentance, and has been faithful to Jesus ever since. I laid hands on Steven the father. I don't remember if he prayed or not. He may have, but he did not become a Christian that night. He thought we were interested in his wife, and told us to take her with us. He, of course, was bombed out of his mind. We prayed with the Gary and Y his sister. I didn't get an impression that anything happened, but I was wrong.

Patsy is a full blood Cherokee Indian. Steven, I think, was part Cherokee. It was hard to tell because one side of his face was destroyed. At the age of 4 years he fell against a red hot wood stove, and that side of his face was terribly damaged. He would try and turn the good side of his face toward people, and he was reasonably handsome on one side and monstrously ugly on the other side. We left after Patsy and her kids prayed.

Don R, Curt B, and I started a home Bible Study and Prayer meeting in the little town nearby. Food was brought in and the meetings became a wonderful success. One evening, Steve S, with the one half burned face, came in, and Curt B responded with a welcome hug and put his face on the damaged side of Steve's face. I still well up with tears when I think about that one act of love. Steve S became a friend and we built a relationship with him. One sunny day in the spring, I heard that Steve told Patsy that he want to see me. He sent for the author. I went out with another evangelist and under the big tree by his trailer house Steve became a Christian. Shortly after that I left for my Island home in Lake Michigan. When I got back to Arkansas, I heard that Steve was killed when his trailer caught fire. Steve is now with the Lord in heaven with a beautiful face on both sides.

As a side issue, the next pastor to come to our church was jealous of the big Bible and prayer meeting in the next town, and he asked me if I was starting a church. My answer was that I had no intentions of starting a church. I asked him if I should close it down. He said yes, and I mistakenly obeyed. The church was growing, and he wrongly thought it was due to his program. What he failed to understand was that the whole middle section in the front pews was filled with the people from the Bible study in the nearby town. These people, without the Bible study and prayer meeting, eventually went to other churches. And my church was back to the same number they had for years. This episode was not a fight between me and the pastor. There was never any raised voices or did I hold any animosity against him. I liked the guy, but I did look for another church where there was a strong outreach. It took me years to find a church that was centered on doing the work of the Lord.

Back to Patsy S and her children. I was in Walmart where I ran into Patsy. We caught up on our families, and then she said that Gary, her son, was a preacher. This was the kid that I prayed with in the trailer house on a hill in Oklahoma years before. She told me where and when he was preaching. My wife and I went out to the church where Gary was holding a service. Before we stepped inside, I could hear Gary's fiery sermon. When we stepped through the door, he stopped preaching. He was silent for a moment. He said, "That man who just walked through the door came to my home and prayed with a 16 year-old Indian boy. That is when I found Christ." Gary devoted the rest of his sermon to me. In fact I was a little embarrassed, but I loved it. I paid not as much attention to the children that night that Patsy became a Christian. Steve eventually trusted me and called for me later to lead him to Christ. The real conversion was Gary who is an awesome preacher, and in a way Gary is one of my replacements in evangelism after I go to my eternal home. Just one little evening going down a dark rutted lane to a trailer sitting on a hill with dogs circling trying to get the courage to bite, and Steve, the father, drunk inside with a loaded shotgun, and all I had to do was get the courage to go inside and lead the family to Jesus. It doesn't get any better than that.

The two previous examples were people that I contacted and led them to Christ. I have no idea how many if any were ahead of me sowing seeds in these people's lives. I assume there were some, but these two families were my spiritual children from start to finish. I was there when the Holy Spirit came and ministered to them in such a way they become Christians and they continued on in the Faith. Most of my evangelical work is carried out as a team where I was aware of many Christian people in their lives before me. Some were at the altar in church. Some were in an airplane. Some were in my engineering classes. Some were in homes. Some were in bars. Some were in the streets.

I taught for 22 years, and 12 of those years, I was in a state university where I could have been reprimanded for my witness. I put the students ahead of my career. In doing so, I still received tenure and after that I could have told the university president to go jump in the lake if I wanted to. Something about me seems funny to people, and they don't get all bent out of shape with my witness. Part of my success is because I start with my testimony. With my testimony told, I become a sinner in their eyes that understands people's problems, and by some process, quit the sin business. No formal Bible talk such as, "Oh God of Abraham, Isaac, and Jacob let thee come into this dog of a sinner's heart." Or something like that.

I can remember Benny. The pastor sent me there because Benny was trying hard to kill himself. I called up Don R, my calling partner, and we went to Benny's home in Arkansas. Benny was drunk and having delirium tremors. He was jerking around so on the floor that I put my knee on his chest to pray for him. Don R and I spent the next few months ministering to Benny. We took him to Mexico with us to build a church. In the meantime, he accepted the Lord, but he would slip and get drunk. I would tell him that if I gave up following Jesus with my first sin, I would have lasted two months at the most. Benny went to church, but he also got drunk on occasion. Finally, I got tired of dealing with him, and I told Don R to take him under his wing. I was frustrated and wanted out of the Benny project. Don R kept at it with love and patience, and finally Benny quit drinking. He became a normal citizen, and he and his wife attended church regularly for sometime.

Benny could not read well, and he never really felt at ease in a group that might ask him to read scripture. He eventually stopped going to church, but I have seen him around. His face shines, and he is sober.

This is a point that we all need to understand. A significant number of people have trouble reading. There was a woman at our church that wanted to take her kids to "kids church". She was asked to fill out a form. She said she changed her mind and brought the wild kids into the sanctuary. The real problem was she could not handle filling out the form. Before asking someone to read or fill out a form, make sure they can read. This is a real problem for a few of people that Christ died for.

Benny's brother was a different story. He also was a drunk and wanted to harm himself. I would witness to Mr. O, Benny's brother, a number of times. The last time I saw him, he was on his hands and knees crawling to his cabin. His German police dog followed him licking the tears running out of his nose. I was right beside him telling him that Jesus loved him. That was the last time I saw Mr. O alive. I tell this non-victorious story because the followers of Christ keep on with success or failure. It made me more determined to see the Holy Spirit save the lost.

Skeeter was another story with mixed results. The first time I met Skeeter was when I called on his friend who was destined to go to prison. They told me later that they were planning a robbery. I gave my witness to both of them. Skeeter said, "I have tried everything else but Jesus." He had been thrown out of his apartment by Gloria his wife. He went home, and I followed. I went in and probably stopped the fight. They would fight, and not just with words. Gloria bragged about doing every sin in the book except she never got into the prostitution business. She was a looker, and you could tell by her dress that she might be available. I gave my testimony, and we all knelt down at their couch. I was praying and after some time, Gloria jumped up shouting. She yelled, "It is gone. It is gone, It is gone." Her burdens were gone, and she jumped around the living room. I turned my attention to Skeeter. He was still at the couch crying. I would pound the cushion as I was on my knees beside him telling him to pray on and ask Jesus to forgive him. I could not help but notice that the tears were running off his nose, and when I hit the cushion, the stream of tears off his nose flipped back and forth. Skeeter asked Jesus to come into his heart.

Skeeter and Gloria came to church regularly. Gloria had a provocative way of walking. She wore a mini-skirt, and she made people look at her. Her walk was uniquely designed to encourage men to lustfully gaze at her. She could not keep her hips from swinging. This was done out of habit. When she accepted Jesus she did not give up some of the world's ways immediately. I actually thought it was funny to be with Skeeter and Gloria in the presence of the church women who put one hand up to cover their open mouths. It takes time for the hard core sinners to follow the modern Christian protocol, and patience and gentleness are needed by older Christians.

I lived almost 40 miles away from the church on a farm in southern Michigan. Skeeter got a job type setting with a company in Jackson, Michigan. I went there with him to round up a mentor to help these new Christians. I found a pastor in a denomination that did reach out. I introduced him to Skeeter and this pastor was supposed to disciple Skeeter and Gloria. I don't know how many times this has happened when I have connected people to a pastor who thought this stuff was outside his job description. The pastor who agreed to take care of Skeeter and Gloria never made any effort to contact them after my first meeting with the pastor.

Gloria got pregnant with twins. They named one of twins Ryan after me. I lost track of them. I found out where they lived. When I went to the address, the house was burned to the ground. A neighbor thought Skeeter burned it down. Although, I do not know where they are at, if they are still alive, or anything about the outcome of their lives. I do know that Skeeter and Gloria will never forget the days we had with each other. I believe they will remember the feeling of being forgiven and in the presence of our Lord and Savior.

One of the engineering students came into my office when I was teaching at John Brown University. This is a Christian college where many believed that these students were from Christian homes and had gone to Church most of their lives. Therefore they must be Christians. I looked at Jim who came into my office for help with homework, and what I heard coming out of my mouth was "You're not a Christian are you?" He smiled and said, "Nope." I witnessed to him privately and also to the whole class that he was taking. Since this was a Christian college, the faculty was encouraged to share Christ in the classroom. Jim graduated, and started an engineering business that was very successful. One day, I got a call from him. He told me that he was a Christian now, and he co-pastored a new church. I hung up the phone and knew that my testimony had not been lost on this young man. He wanted me to know that he now was a disciple of Jesus Christ.

This Christian university required students to attend chapel twice a week. The quality and spirituality of the speakers varied. I was adamant about giving the students a chance to respond. In other words, how about an old fashion altar call. It went over the faculty and administrations heads. "After all our students are probably all saved." I brought up the retirement plan and altar calls at every faculty meeting. One week they had an "altar call". Young college students got up from all over the auditorium and went forward. There was standing room only in front of the chapel. I didn't count them, but there were from 50 to 100 kids repenting and asking Jesus for salvation.

Witnessing is for everyone. There is the false doctrine that evangelism is not their calling. They are teachers or something else. It is for everyone and to be done everywhere. Acts 1:8 states it clearly what we need to do.

**Acts 1:8 "But ye shall receive power, after that the Holy Ghost is come upon you and ye shall be witnesses unto me both in Jerusalem, and in all Judea, and in Samaria, and unto the uttermost parts of the earth."**

Many clergy do not get in the streets for one reason or another. A few apparently think that they are above street evangelism, and many of them physically do not have the time. I remember when I pastored a small circuit for the Methodist Church in northern Ohio. I was working on my master's degree in mechanical engineering at the University of Toledo with a teaching assistantship and serving the two churches part-time. The churches were formerly Evangelical United Brethren that were forced into the Methodist denomination due to a merger of the EUB with the Methodist. The one church did not like the change and voted to leave the denomination. Some of their decision was based on the liberal politics of the denomination. I was caught in the middle of the fight, and I tried to stay neutral. Perhaps that was some of the problems that I had with my replacement pastor for the church that decided to stay with the Methodists. I went to the parsonage and knocked on the door. During my year and a half I had called on everybody while being a teaching assistant and attending the University of Toledo. In fact, in the rebellious church, we called on everybody in the township, and the church grew and prospered. I had a large list of names, and I thought it was very valuable for the next pastor. I went to the parsonage and knocked. My replacement came to the door. He opened the door a crack. The crack was about two inches at the most. I told him through the crack that I had a notebook of names of prospects and members of the church. He said he was going to seminary and would not call on anyone. In other words, he had not the slightest interest in doing anything except preaching on Sundays. He didn't want my notebook, and quickly slammed the door.

My general rule is to allow everyone, including myself one fit a month. This new guy just had his allowed fit for the month. So I did not even get upset. In fact, I thought it was funny in a way. If I would have said "boo" I'm sure he would have fainted. The more I think about it, he seemed frightened of me.

Some of the problem may have been that the denominational leadership may have wired him in on me because they somehow blamed me for the loss of the conservatives in the church that left the denomination. However, if I were the pastor, and I had replaced Adolf Hitler, I would have paid money for that calling list. My conclusion is, there are pastors, few I hope, that are not interested in seeing people saved if they have to do it. One pastor friend of mine said that the people invite folks to church and then the pastor gets them saved in the service. Of course the Holy Spirit does the saving, but I knew what he meant. His church was without an altar call or any other form of evangelism. I guess we are back to the "be good and they will come to Jesus" idea.

# CHAPTER 12: VISIONS

Unbelief is the malady that resides in people inside and outside the church. They missed the miracles. They missed the presence of the Holy Spirit. Some of them are in churches that deny the power of the Holy Spirit. Since the Bible claims : ***Joel 2:28 "And it shall come to pass afterwards that, I will pour out my spirit on all flesh; and your sons and daughters shall prophesy, and your old men shall dream dreams, your young men shall see visions." People should see visions and have dreams.***

Visions are a miracle from God to communicate important things to His people. As I write this, I can feel the unbelief rising. I can see the results if someone stood up in the congregation and said, "I had a vision last night ... "Ah, sir let's talk about it after the service." To validate Joel 2:28, I interviewed Jack A. Here is his story from my notes and a hand written paper by Jack to correct some details:

## *Jack Apple...*

"It was on a rainy October 19, 2002 when my family and I were headed to a funeral in Oklahoma. My two grandbabies were in the back of our 98 Ford Windstar. My son and his wife were in the middle two seats of the 6 passenger van. My first wife was driving and I was sitting beside her in the front seat. She came upon an intersection and failed to see the stop sign. She proceeded to cross the highway without stopping. There was a gravel lane on the other side. A young driver approached the intersection doing 67 miles per hour in a 45 mile per hour zone. He approached from the left. The two vehicles met at the intersection. The other vehicle "T-Boned" our vehicle just behind the driver's seat. We ended up on the far side near the gravel lane hitting a tree on the right. I was knocked unconscious. The airbag broke my nose and teeth. There was glass and blood all over me. My son removed people from the smoking vehicle and laid them out on the ground. The emergency rescue people came and started working on the two babies first. Erin was 3 years old and Brittney was 4 years old. They put a tarp over the children while they were working on them to save their lives. They were taken to the local hospital in Tahlequah, Oklahoma, and then they were all transferred to St. Francis Hospital in Tulsa, Oklahoma."

(Jack A proofed my description of what happened, and this came from his hand written paper next:) "There at the Tahlequah City Hospital they told me that my grandbabies didn't make it. They were in the morgue, and I could see them if I liked. Then I had to identify them by their dresses they were wearing. Also, I had to tell them who all to notify. The nurse asked me if I would like something for the pain. She left the room and came back later with some medication. She gave me three shots and the third shot put me out. I was hurt, but more from the heart than anywhere else. Later I was awakened by my ex-sister in law picking glass from my face and body. Then they said they were going to transfer all of us to Saint Francis Hospital in Tulsa, but said I could see my Grandbabies before I left, so I did. Then we were all taken to Saint Francis in Tulsa where later I was released. I stayed there because my first ex-wife and son and daughter-in-law were still there, which was on a Saturday. The next day our assistant and lead pastor came to visit. I was in the waiting room when they showed up. They came to visit. We talked and then we had prayer. When we were done, I looked up and my grandbabies' pictures were there on the wall in front of me. They were very beautiful angels with a very gorgeous background. That is a sign that there is a heaven and a God that has control over everything that happens around us in this world.

"We all bowed our heads and prayed. Everyone prayed. When we were finished, I looked up, and on the wall was the Vision. The Vision was my two babies standing side by side in the dresses they had on before the accident. They were standing looking back at me with a blue background and over their heads were halos. I knew they were in heaven."[xv]

Jack said he was with them when they came into the world, and he was with them when they went out of the world.

He told me the first girl was born on January 1, 1998. The second girl was born in September of 1999. They died in October 19, 2002. This interview was held on April 28, 2015. The Vision occurred almost 13 years ago, and it is still vivid in Jack's mind.

I asked him what the memories of this vision did for him. Jack said, "There is a heaven, and the girls will be there when I get there. The girls were not our girls. They were just loaned to us for a time." Here are deceased girls with a present address of God's Heaven.

Some might think that Jack's vision was actually the result of all the trauma. Without the trauma there would be no vision. Or Jack's mind made up what he wanted to see. The next visions were not under trauma, stress, or anything that could explain the visions. The Bible tells us clearly that visions and dreams will occur in our life. Believe it and toss out any concept that nothing happens spiritually in this scientific world.

## *The Author's Visions:*

A Vision is a very vivid picture that you see clearly for years. It never goes away. It is always there. The details are present years later such as color, position, and a message in the vision. I have had three visions in my 80 years of walking on this earth. My first Vision was to help me, an atheist at the time, to believe in the unseen world. My second Vision was to redirect the work of my life toward God and away from the secular. The last Vision for me was to give a message to a group of people in a home church on what I saw. It was the flaw in the peoples lives that hindered them from moving into solutions for their lives. This vision is the fundamental reason for this book. Christians must open gates for those fenced into their godless world.

## *The First Vision:*

About sixty years ago, an atheist, the author, not believing in anything, was dragged to the altar by aggressive evangelical people who wanted to see this sinner saved. That was me the sinner that complied with Jesus words in Revelations. **Revelation 3:16 "So then because thou are lukewarm, and neither cold or hot, I will spue thee out of my mouth."**

I turned and looked up at this three dimensional vision hanging to the left side of this globe light suspended from the cathedral ceiling. A black chain with a globe light attached at the end had this angel to the left side of the chain and leaning 15 degrees or more to the left from my perspective. I will call it an angel for lack of a better word. This angel was looking at me and was mute. He or she was life size. The angel probably did not have a gender, but for the discussion, I will call the being male. He had long brown shoulder length hair that was straight. There were no curls. The hair on his forehead was cut into bangs. He had large brown eyes. He looked straight at me, but there was no conversation between us. His clothing was also dark brown and it had a course weave that looked like burlap. At that moment, I knew there was more to my world than what I could see. I came apart at the seams, and cried like a baby over my sinful life. This was the baptism of repentance that was the first step in becoming a Christian.

I had been baptized when I was 8 years old because my father, who was going off to war, wanted to see his children baptized. I'm not sure why he did this. He was not a Christian. Except maybe he felt obligated to cover the spiritual requirements as he knew them before he went to war where he might end up dead, but personally, I had no idea why I was baptized. I felt nothing except a little apprehension about get dunked under water. It was years later that I was baptized again as a believer at the age of 79 in Font Lake on Beaver Island, Michigan. It was not a necessary act except I wanted to fulfill all righteousness. It was symbolic in a powerful way.

Oh, I believe Jesus was conceived by the Holy Spirit inside the egg of the virgin Mary. He grew up from infant to boy to man. Jesus was a pure sinless person. He was handsome and could probably run a four minute mile. Since God created this perfect lamb, His flesh was flawless. Any ugliness came after evil men beat on Him. His flesh, which would be offered up as the supreme sacrifice, apparently did not possess the Holy Spirit yet. The Spirit had not entered into Jesus until that time when John baptized Him. Then things began. I cannot help believe that this very vivid scene was put in the Bible for a major reason. I think that an encounter with the Holy Spirit who enters and resides inside us is the key to a successful ministry. That may explain all the fallen Christians who believed and were saved, but they lacked the power to overcome temptation and as a result fell. Maybe this is why Christians do not see signs, wonders, healings, and powerful conversion is because they have not been baptized in the Holy Spirit. A person cannot hold Traditional views that are wrong and expect to get anywhere in God's kingdom.

Maybe we do not have dreams and visions because of our baby status in the Lord. All we have to do is to believe in the Lord Jesus Christ to be saved. Baptism for the one thief on the cross was not available, but Jesus told him that today he would be with the Lord in paradise. Water baptism then is not necessarily a requirement for salvation, but it is a powerful statement of the intent to follow Jesus Christ. There is the Baptism in water, which is a second baptism.

John 14 is full of the concept of the Holy Trinity living inside us. In my humble opinion, this does not come from a trip to the altar or belief. There is no question that believing will be the ticket to heaven unless you happen to be the Devil who also believes, but if one wants to take other souls along, it take the miraculous third baptism similar to what happened to Jesus when he came up out of the water in the arms of John the Baptist.

***John 14: 10-17 "Don't you believe that I am in the Father, and that the Father is in me? The words I say to you I do not speak on my own authority. Rather, it is the Father, living in me, who is doing his work. Believe me when I say that I am in the Father and the Father is in me; or at least believe on the evidence of the works themselves. Very truly I tell you, whoever believes in me will do the works I have been doing, and they will do even greater things than these, because I am going to the Father. And I will do whatever you ask in my name, so that the Father may be glorified in the Son. You may ask me for anything in my name, and I will do it. If you love me, keep my commands. And I will ask the Father, and he will give you another advocate to help you and be with you forever— the Spirit of truth. The world cannot accept him, because it neither sees him nor knows him. But you know him, for he lives with you and will be in you."***(KJV)

I put these thoughts in the middle of this chapter on visions, because after the first vision of the angel hanging in the air near the globe light in church to get me to believe, I did not have another vision until after I was baptized in the Holy Spirit. Since that time I have had two visions, and my wife has had one very vivid spiritual dream.

## *Second Vision:*

The second vision was a picture of a beautiful landscape with an old door frame rotted on the lower left side. The door frame was centered over a path winding up in the hills. It was very clear, and I can see the scene now. I knew exactly what it meant, and what my reaction to it should be.

I live on an island in the middle of northern Lake Michigan on one of the seven inland lakes on the island. My wife and I spend the summer and part of fall on Beaver Island. We camped out for 4 months in the 1970's and the Ryan family built a log house. It took 35 years to totally finish the cabin. We added a sun porch, and I needed a garage. So we built a garage on the next lot with an apartment above the garage. The apartment came out very nice, and Sue and I moved into it. This left the cabin empty. There is a demand for cabins for tourists to rent in the summer. We listed the cabin for rent on the Chamber of Commerce web site. The first year we were pleased that the cabin was fully rented over the spring and summer. The rent money partially paid for the taxes, insurance, and expenses.

The vision came about after the first year of renting the cabin. Since we lived next door, there was the opportunity to witness to the renters, but God wanted more. The vision of the door frame with the left side partially rotted became clear. The rotted door frame lead to a path that apparently lead to paradise. A similar picture is shown next. It was the same concept as my vision. (The picture is reproduced here.) The rotted door frame represented what would happen to all my worldly goods. Everything including my flesh will rot away into dust. The cabin should be used as a ministry, which was clear.

We are making the cabin open to people who need to get away to a beautiful place to find God or find themselves or just to relax. It is over a thousand miles from our winter home in Arkansas where we have people in our ministry that could use a week on Beaver Island. This creates a cost problem for our recovering addicts in Arkansas to get to Beaver Island that God hopefully will solve.

## *The Third Vision:*

The third vision was simple and very clear. It was an old fence with weeds and grass growing up through the wire rectangles. What could an old fence mean? Since the vision happened right before I entered a home meeting, I knew what the message meant. Everyone in that meeting of 6 people had some type of fence or restriction that prevented them from being all they could be. At the time, I did not include myself, but a year later, I recognized that I had built a few fences of my own.

I shared the vision that produced a prophesy about people staying inside their comfortable zone. This vision eventually made more of an impression on me than it had when I have shared this fence vision with others. Fences are a barrier stopping people from being all they can be. At first, I really didn't think too much about the fence, but as time passed, the simple fence vision has become very important. The drug and alcohol addicts are fenced in with addiction. Even though they tell me they hate their life, there is a certain comfort to staying where they are. The unknown is scary. The obese are addicted to food. Beautiful people that are addicted to food go from being desirable to being very undesirable. The fence to break through is eating stuff that tastes good and lots of it. There are no fat people in concentration camps. It certainly is not worth proclaiming to the world that they are addicted to food, and it is hard not to judge them harshly for their addiction. Other addictions do not expose the person to such public scrutiny.

My personal fences: I finally figured out one of the fences in my life, and I started to tear it down. I was constantly trying to team up with other Christians and pastors to come along side their ministry. That never worked. There was always conflict of some kind. I had a deep desire to find the lost and even though I was willing to subject myself to a leader younger and less experienced, it rarely happened. I apparently threaten folks with my open style. It is apparent that my wife and I need to follow the Lord independently of other peoples' ministry.

My wife and I started Earth Mission a mission agency that initially created appropriate technology for missionaries, and we developed cottage industries for the indigent people in our ministry. Earth Mission grew and took on the responsibility of financing projects and missionaries. The Board began to function like a real agency. They brought into Earth Mission a director who was the smoothest person I have ever known. He seemed very knowledgeable. His fence was to follow some other mission agencies protocol. He wanted to take total control of the finances that belong to the missionaries. He allegedly proposed a $2000 limit after receiving and reviewing the request from the missionaries. This was another fence created by a well meaning director to have his way in the operation of Earth Mission. Today, Earth Mission operates effectively with the funds received going directly for the intended projects. So the fence that I built was to give someone else control over something God had ordained. This trouble came from not understanding the scope of the ministry. The director was apparently trying to copy what other agencies were doing, and they basically didn't understand that the Board, was there to support the missionaries, and we were getting our direction from the missionaries in the field. The old director was not evil. He just didn't understand where Earth Mission was heading, and he felt content to stay inside the traditional fence of board control of missionaries.

The person that was directing Earth Mission at that time left, and he went to another overseas project related to Earth Mission. I just heard that he closed this hospital and gave the equipment and property away. The people that had jobs at the hospital joined the unemployed in that country, and the blind no longer have operations to restore their sight. I am even angry as I write and think about this decision. I did not bring this person on board Earth Mission. He came after I retired. Leadership must be run by the Holy Spirit and not with what appears to be "good ideas" or "what is hard" is avoided. Not everything that happened is this Alexander the coppersmith's fault. (The past director.) Some of it was very hard to do.

My next mission agency was designed to prevent the fence that developed with Earth Mission. Acts One Eight International, relatively new 501 (c) (3) organization, ministers to felons, substance abusers, and lost souls. We have an Executive Board that is commissioned for life, and an Operational Board that has a one year tenure, and they can be removed or continued on the Operational Board by action of the Executive Board.

**Using visions:** When I make evangelical calls, I usually describe my vision in the old EUB church of the angel looking down at me. The angel with the burlap looking clothes, straight brown hair with bangs, and brown piercing eyes staring at me has reaped souls for the kingdom of God. I told this story recently to a couple in their home. This couple lived together without marriage for years. The woman was an alcoholic, and the man had been in prison. After I left, my testimony touched this couple through the Holy Spirit. They started attending a church with a very good pastor. They are maturing Christians. They are married, and they recently returned from a short term mission trip to the American Indians.

Visions do produce prophetic statements that God wants told, and visions increase faith in the unbelievers and the person seeing the vision. Visions are useful and practical. Visions are a wonderful tool, and visions are available today.

# CHAPTER 13: THE SCRIPTURES NOT READ

There are scriptures that many people and denominations fail to read or understand, particularly when the scriptures are outside their denominational or personal beliefs. It is hard to understand why anyone would exclude the scriptures that have the potential of reaching the truth and correcting their doctrinal error. Is it pride? Is it burdensome to follow? Wouldn't everyone want to follow the truth of what Christ said? Whatever the reasons, leaping over scriptures that could prove some of their theories wrong is a common practice, and believing something false weakens the person holding the untrue concept.

I would not be so critical if it involved some obscure concept that is of little importance. There is a denomination that makes a big deal of how a person is baptized. They feel that when Christ died He fell forward. Therefore when people are baptized, they must be baptized like Jesus' death. They baptize their converts forward rather than rearward as most churches do. Forward makes a lot of practical sense because a person does not get water up his or her nose. To me, the big insensitive guy, it does not matter much. Or the question will be asked, "How were you baptized?" Sprinkled? Or should you have been immersed like Jesus? Or what did the person say when you went under?

Personally, I do not care what the person is saying doing the baptizing. When I was eight years old, I was put completely under the water backwards. This was before I was saved. I had no idea what the guy baptizing was saying or why he was doing it. I could not hear. This is also an issue in some denominations by what is said by the person doing the baptizing. What did the person say when putting someone under? Was it, "I baptize you in the name of the Father, Son, and Holy Ghost." Or as Peter said in Acts, "I baptize you in the name of Jesus"? If the exact words are important then the validity of the baptismal act depends on the words of someone else, and not the person dealing with God. This is also an issue for some denominations. How important is all this stuff? The reader can decide. It does seem to me that dunking the folks completely under would eliminate an easy conversion. Maybe the nominally dedicated Christians would be eliminated by submersion.

I realized that my first baptism was based on my Father's desire to see his children baptized before he went off to war. I knew it was not necessary for me to be baptized again because I was baptized long before I was saved. It was my father's decision and not mine. Maybe that is why I was baptized again in Font Lake on Beaver Island at 80 years of age. I did not do it for any necessary requirement. I just wanted to do everything right. Since the thief on the cross could not be baptized, yet he was going to be with Christ in paradise, the act itself of how baptism is done is not critical in my mind. The act of repenting for sins is importantly symbolized by baptism.

However, when the issue is the Holy Spirit, this is a different matter. Believing that the Holy Spirit lives and works in us today is extremely important. Some say all the miracles stopped with the death of the apostles. This cannot be proven with scripture or history. Some say when that which is perfect has come, tongues, prophecy , and knowledge will stop. What is perfect except the Lord Jesus Christ? The supporters of the work of the Holy Spirit in our present time believe that when we are faced with perfection and standing before Jesus there is no need for the tools used on the earth in the past. Those who do not believe in the active working of the Holy Spirit in this age believe that the Bible, in one of the translations, is perfection on earth. So at least between the time that the Bible was assembled and published, the perfect had not yet come. The canon took time. There was and is a difference between the accepted versions by different branches of Christianity. So tongues, prophecy, and knowledge would logically continue until all the people had the perfect scriptures available with this common view. That alone would conflict with the concept that all the miracles, tongues, prophecy, and knowledge stopped with the apostles. Knowledge certainly did not. Not everybody has the scripture in their language today. It took time to put the Bible together. The reader should study how the Bible was assembled. Go to Wikipedia under the "Development of the Christian canon" for a quick review. This was a process that took years, and there are some minor variations in the product produced called the Bible for different groups. None of this makes sense to me that some people would take one of the versions of the Bible and make it almost an idol by assuming this is the perfection talked about in 1 Corinthians 13. It is not. The perfection is the second coming of our Lord and Savior Jesus Christ, and the Bible is the word of God that we follow. It is what the old guys did and heard. We do nothing outside of the scripture, but to say that it is something to worship is off base.

No, I do not minimize the importance of the scriptures. It is our guide and director of what we do and why we do it. The New Testament, in particular, is as perfect as man can create perfection through the Holy Spirit. My wife and I just finished Ecclesiastes and felt that Solomon was writing about his failure to see the God of the universe. Meaningless, every thing is meaningless. Nothing new under the sun. He really felt bad about the impending death of everyone, particularly himself. This is one great work to see what not to do, and it should be part of the Bible. The forty years of wandering is also valuable, and what happened afterwards is just as valuable, and it is what God wanted in the Bible. But, it was not meant to be an idol that we bow down and worship. The Bible simply tells what others did and didn't do. It is a writing to us to tell us what we can do and what we should be doing. The book of Acts is still being written today. Today's Christian should be writing Acts 29 with the same tools that the first church had, which include tongues, prophesy, healing, signs and wonders.

The other reality of the Bible is the recording of persecutions. If we are not trying to "fit in" with the world, we should read some of the persecution the early church endured. In fact we are seeing increased persecutions of Christians in our time. In the Middle East,

Christians are being beheaded. In the USA, Christians are not being helped by the main stream media, which is an understatement. There is a growing trend of opposition to Christians around the world that will someday show its ugly head as violent persecution. Christians should beware of how they vote. Think about what the candidates support and vote accordingly. I have friends that I ask if they support abortions, same sex marriage, and prohibiting school prayer to name a few, and they don't, but they still vote for someone that supports all this evil stuff because the candidate is for the poor or they have always voted for that party or some other reason. I do not get it.

## *Homosexuals:*

Look at the homosexual issues. I personally know Christians that are for "same sex marriage". They have to ignore many scriptures related to the subject. The media is treating homosexuals as a civil rights issue. Just for a little fun on the author's part, how far does a reader have to jump over the following scriptures:

*Romans 1:26 "For this cause God gave them up into vile affections; for even their women did change the natural use that which is against nature:"*(KJV)

*Romans 1:27 " And likewise also the men, leaving the natural use of the women, burned in their lust one toward another; men with men working that which is unseemly, and receiving in themselves that recompense of their error which was meet."*(KJV)

*1 Corinthians 6:9 "know ye not that the unrighteous shall not inherit the kingdom of God: Be not deceived; neither fornicators, nor idolaters, nor adulterers, no effeminate, nor abusers of themselves with mankind."* (KJV)

***1 Corinthians 7:2 "Nevertheless, to avoid fornication, let every man have his own wife, and let every women have her own husband."*** (KJV)

This is what the Bible says. So how do we deal with homosexuals? Love them. Develop relationships with them so that when the day comes when they become sick of their sins, they will call on Christians to lead them to the Master. As I frequently say, don't try to change people with your own moral code. Change them with the power of the Holy Spirit. Christ does the changing. Christians carry the message.

The point in even including the anti gay scriptures is to prove many Christians just get back, get a run, and leap over scriptures that they don't like. There are plenty that either don't know what the Bible says or they do the proverbial leap across these scriptures.

The Holy Spirit is needed in our time more than ever. All the gifts are needed in our present age. Without the direct work of the Holy Spirit now, the church will go nowhere. There will be nothing to show for their effort. All the people that believe in the power of the Holy Spirit now are either right or wrong. By the evidence presented here and elsewhere through the Holy Spirit, He is alive and well living inside many Christians, and He is using His power and ability in His believers. We are seeing signs, wonders, and miracles through the Holy Spirit in the Lord's disciples. Many speak in tongues. Many prophecy. Many see people healed through the power of the Holy Spirit. Many see visions. All of this is through the Holy Spirit. Why would the God who created everything remove the tools we need to follow His Great Commission of winning men, women, boys, and girls to Jesus in this age?

Read the scriptures that you may have missed. I start with the women's role in church because there have been church splits over the topic. Let us see what all the scripture says about women's involvement in church.

## *Women's Role in Church:*

The scripture addresses the role of women in the church if the reader would not stop on one scripture and develop a doctrine without reading the rest. There are three scriptures needed to understand the role of women in church. First, start with how church, as we call it, is supposed to be held. It did not start with a pastor being the supreme leader in the church doing all the talking. What Christianity has evolved into is the people come to church where there is a strange format compared to the early church. There are three hymns, one special, and the sermon. There are other little side things that happen, but in a typical church that is all there is to that to quote Forrest Gump. The people participate to the extent of listening. In other words, not only are the women to remain quiet, but so are the men and the children. The following is how church was held in the New Testament:

*1 Corinthians 14:5 (King James Version) "I would that ye all spake with tongues, but rather that ye prophesied: for greater is he that prophesieth than he that speaketh with tongues, except he interpret, that the church may receive edifying."* (KJV)

*1 Corinthians 14: 27-33 [27]" If any man speak in an unknown tongue, let it be by two, or at the most by three, and that by course; and let one interpret. [28] But if there be no interpreter, let him keep silence in the church, and let him speak to himself and to God. [29] Let the prophets speak two or three, and let the other judge. [30] If anything be revealed to another that sitteth by, let the first hold his peace. [31] For ye may all prophesy one by one, that all may learn, and all may be comforted.[32] And the spirits of the prophets are subject to the prophets. [33] For God is not the author of confusion, but of peace."*KJV)

*Acts 14: 5 "I would that ye all spake with tongues, but rather that ye prophesied"* ...(KJV)

***Acts 14: 18 " I thank my God, I speak in tongues more than ye all".*** (KJV)

***I Thessalonians 5: 19-20 "Quench not the Spirit. Despise not prophesying."*** (KJV)

One question, does the above look like our church meetings? In other words, we are not following the New Testament church as they conducted church. Another scripture leaped over. We have moved away from this format to one where the pastor is the key speaker. He speaks, and we, the lay people listen week after week. There is usually a singing of the old hymns, a responsive Bible reading, and maybe a special song by some talented person who gets his or her 3 to 4 minutes of fame. Most churches do not have an outreach at all. Emotion of any kind is ruled out of order. Many churches have never seen a conversion. They cling to what they believe like their denomination held all the truth. Many times these beliefs conflict with Bible. If the procedures in the church or the ability of the person who holds the control of the church isn't what the listener can tolerate for an hour, they leave and seek other churches. Basically, church changing is like the game of musical chairs. When the music stops, the person grabs a chair in another church.

In the next section, I have listed scripture that many just skip over or claim a part of their beliefs without including other biblical references such as the role of women in church.

***1 Corinthians 14:34: "Let your women keep silence in the churches, for it is not permitted unto them to speak, but they are commanded to be under obedience as also saith the law." (Also 1 Timothy 2: 11-12)*** (KJV)

By the Holy Spirit we are taught right and wrong, and I have known that many men marry up. In other words, their wives are more intelligent and capable in some cases than the husbands. It seems without logic that God wants to silence women. For the specific churches Paul was talking about, the women should shut up because this was a problem church caused by women. But what about Philip and his four virgins who prophesied? You cannot prophesy unless it is accomplished in church. Here is the counter to **1 Corinthians: 14:34:**

**Acts 21: 8-9 "And the next day we that were of Paul's company departed, and came unto Caesarea; and we entered into the house of Philip the evangelist, which was one of the seven, and abode with him. [9] And the same man had four daughters, virgins, which did prophesy. [10] And as we tarried there many days, ..."(KJV)**

Note they stayed there with Philip many days. Paul and Luke, the author of Acts, were there. It was so many days that the exact count may have been lost in the mind of the writer Luke. It can be safely assumed that church was held while the entourage stayed with Philip. It can be safely assumed that they found out about the daughters in the service. If you prophesy, the mouth is open and words come out. In other words where Paul had the women mute and check with their husbands at home in one problem church, Philip's daughter did not remain silent in church. At least if women have a message to give from the Lord, speak out in church. I believe it is broader than that. Women supported Jesus financially during his ministry. Women were the first to proclaim his resurrection. Women are the equals of men, and problem people in church may be required to stay silent regardless of gender. The author is basically mute in church services unless asked to preach or share something. Men and women are mute in today's modern church.

If there was such a thing as a pecking order in the first church, Philip was appointed to his position by the apostles. He was one of the seven that included Stephen who was stoned to death with the help of Paul. Paul was converted on the road to Damascus. Philip had some status in the early church, and this scripture should not be ignored on Philip's four virgin daughters that gave prophesy in church.

***Acts 2:17** quoted "And it shall come to pass in the last days, saith God, I will pour out of my Spirit upon all flesh, and your sons and your daughters shall prophesy, and your young men shall see visions, and your old men shall dream dreams. [18] And on my servants and on my handmaidens I will pour out in those days of my Spirit, and they shall prophesy:"*(KJV)

This scripture in **Acts 2:17** and its source in Joel should be read and believed. Where are the daughters supposed to prophesy if not in church?

If you are in a church that restricts women from speaking change the practice to keep with the Bible and common sense. Women can teach Sunday school in churches where they cannot hold leadership roles or speak in the sanctuary. How stupid is that?

What is even more interesting is that the women issue was prevalent in the early church. Montanus, a very successful charismatic, used women as part of ministry. Many of his faithful followers were women, and in 170 AD, the church made a stand against women being in leadership roles. They dared to teach, dispute, carry out exorcisms and performed cures, and baptized. A large portion of the church banned women from doing any ministerial duties. In my opinion, this was another step downward in developing a powerless church, and it shows that some of this stuff against women was cultural at the time. Get over it men!

## *The Holy Spirit:*

The whole Christian experience eventually is the involvement with and through the Holy Spirit. Few teach about this person, the Holy Spirit, who lives inside all that are totally committed to following the Lord. The Holy Spirit is our source of power. In John 14, the indwelling of the Holy Spirit is well defined by Jesus.

*John 14: 16-20[16]" And I will pray the Father and he shall give you another Comforter, that he may abide with you for ever, [17] Even the Spirit of truth; whom the world cannot receive, because it seeth him not, neither knoweth him: but ye know him; for he dwelleth with you and shall be in you. [18] I will not leave you comfortless: I will come to you. [19] Yet a little while, and the world seeth me no more; but ye see me because I live, ye shall live also. [20] At that day ye shall know that I am in my Father, and ye in me, and I in you."*(KJV)

From verse 17 of John 14, we can see that the Holy Spirit dwells with us and eventually shall be in us. There are two positions of the Holy Spirit. The first is near us, and the second is in us. From verse 20, at that day, we will know that Jesus is in the Father and we are in Jesus and Jesus is in us. There will be a distinct day when this will happen, and we will know that the Holy Spirit is not now just beside us, but He will be in us. The day is not the first day we believed and were saved. It is a special day. The old Methodists called it sanctification. Others call it being filled or baptized with the Holy Spirit, which should cause some emotional expression. Some speak in tongues. Some feel the powering of God in their lives. The reaction to the infilling of the Holy Spirit is probably different in every individual, but it is a point of change where love begins to reign in the believer's life. It is a place where the sinful life is left behind, and love reigns in our hearts, and this is played out in how we act.

Assume that a room represents a life. When we are born, the room is empty. As time goes on, we add stuff to the room. Good and bad things are added to the room. The good are things that make the occupant comfortable. The bad things come from worldly sin. Usually, the bad things are something that the scripture prohibits or something that we have been taught by the Holy Spirit that is appalling.

Simple people's lives follow the ones in the movies and television.

The "F" word is freely used. The men fail to shave and have the grubby look of the movie stars in this age. In most love stories, the boys and girls move in and have sex before marriage, which is freely practiced by the movie watchers. The homosexuals are honored. The Christians are undesirable jerks. Violence is a solver of problems. Watching porn is a normal activity. The evidence is seen in the proverbial room with magazines and television playing the latest porn movie. The use of drugs is evident in the room. The contents of the room speak to the condition of the person.

When an individual looks into the room and sees what has happened, repentance should follow. In the ideal situation, the persons see themselves as sinners. There is not the typical defense of why they did it: "Well everybody is doing it." Or "I had a very bad childhood." So our prototype person represented by the room full of good and bad feels terrible about what has happened in his or her life. Tears are poured out freely, and he or she follows the tradition of water baptism. They may have always believed in God. The Devil believes also. But something has changed. They get a glimpse of Jesus Christ. They buy a new Bible or dust off the old one, and they get a picture of Jesus knocking on a door. They may know that Christ did knock and they opened up the door to their room. Christ comes in and tells them to get rid of this worldly stuff. The Lord leaves, but they put up the picture of Him knocking on a door. The man or woman go through the room deciding what will be put out at the curb for the trash pickup. Some of it goes. But during the day, they see the junk piled at the curb. Some of it is returned to the room. There begins a process of taking sin in and tossing it out. In and out with the sin. Since the room is so much better than it was, the people are happy. The happy people do attend church and their church says that people sin daily, and there is no complete cure for the dilemma. Grace will be applied and Jesus forgives. The folks sometimes realize that the room is still not clean. The yearning comes and goes to remove everything sinful. They are reassured by their pastor that what they have experienced is normal and they now are Christians, and they are. However, they lack spiritual power, and are caught up with one question: "Is there more?"

In their research for more, a reliable person tells them "there is more". They search through prayer and reading God's word for the answer. After a time, they hear a knock on the door to the room. The Holy Spirit has come visiting. He points to the remaining worldly stuff and says, "If you want Me to live in here for the rest of your lives allow me, through your faith, to cleanse the room. I will live here. I will guide you. I will teach you. The people respond with "Yes, come in." The room is cleaned, and the people have exactly what the Bible says: [**Galatians 5:22 "But the fruit of the Spirit is love, joy, peace, longsuffering, gentleness, goodness, faith."**(KJV)

There will be a few readers that conclude the author is saying that a Christian does not necessarily get the Holy Spirit's fullness when he or she is saved, and they may think this borders on heresy. What does our guide, the Bible, say about this.

**Acts 19: 1-7 [1] "And it came to pass that while Apollos was at Corinth, Paul having passed through the upper coast came to Ephesus: and finding certain disciples, [2] He said unto them, Have ye received the Holy Ghost since ye believed? And they said unto him, We have not so much as heard whether there be any Holy Ghost. [3] And he said unto them, Unto what then were ye baptized? And they said, Unto John's baptism. [4] Then said Paul, John verily baptized with the baptism of repentance, saying unto the people, that they should believe on him which should come after him, that is on Christ Jesus. [5] When they heard this, they were baptized in the name of the Lord Jesus. [6] And when Paul had laid his hands upon them, the Holy Ghost came on them; and they spake with tongues and prophesied. [7] And all the men were about twelve."**(KJV)

This is pretty plain. There were three steps in this scripture. First they believed; then they were baptized, and finally they were filled with the Holy Spirit. The people of Acts 19:1-7 believed. Since the scriptures say if you believe you will be saved. To be effective in this world, you must be filled with the Holy Spirit. I believe that is why the modern church seems so weak. One trip to the altar may or may not result in believing in the Lord. How weak is weak in new Christians?

After I believed and saw a vision, I would not go out and call on a person the church had targeted, and tell them about Jesus. I could not do it. No way was I going to go out and knock on this guy's door and tell him about the Lord I had just met. This whole concept of doing what Jesus said to do with his lost sheep was beyond me. I did not have the Holy Spirit's power to work with then. After I received the power of the Holy Spirit, I would face the Devil and try to discourage him from tempting humanity. I went from a shivering coward to a person who was unafraid and unashamed of Jesus. When people hear some of my testimonies, they do not rejoice, but they come up with excuses why they cannot do that. Some even get mad. We have a men's breakfast on Beaver Island and two of us share what happened evangelically in Arkansas. The reaction was the pastor of one church wished that Larry R and the author would not come to the event because of our success stories out of Arkansas.

Living without the fullness of the Holy Spirit is synonymous to going to Afghanistan without a rifle, body armor, or training. Why would God take away our weapons of spiritual warfare when we have as many obstacles as the first church to winning the world? It make no sense, defies logic, and ignores history. Most of all, no one can prove this taking away of weapons is from the Bible.

To investigate the truth about the Holy Spirit refer to Jack Deere's book: "Surprised by the voice of God", and Robert Morris' book: "The God I never knew". These scholars came out of the dispensation seminaries that taught that all the power of the Holy Spirit stopped with the apostles.

## *Divorce:*

Here is another topic where the scriptures are ignored.

***Mark 10: 11-12 "And he saith unto them, Whosoever shall put away his wife, and marry another, committeth adultery against her. [12] And if a woman shall put away her husband, and be married to another, she committeth adultery."*** (KJV)

***Matthew 19:9 " And I say unto you, Whosoever shall put away his wife, except it be for fornication, and shall marry another, committeth adultery, and whoso marrieth her which is put away doth commit adultery."*** (KJV)

One of my proof readers added a hand written note to this manuscript that said what about MB and then I thought about JR. These two women can walk on water. They are fine Christian women. One of them had a first husband that was mentally ill, and the other married for the first time to a man divorced multiply times. Both women married outstanding Christian men that had been divorced. The "not to judge" statement in the Bible is there for a reason. What they did is against what the Bible commands us to do. It was not an ideal decision. However, I also know that if they thought it was a sinful move to marry a divorced man that Jesus was asked to forgive them. If you would ask the Lord about the marriage, He has put that into the great abyss of His forgetfulness. He would say, "What are you talking about?"

I happen to be led by the Holy Spirit when I found Sue even though I was unaware of His leading at the time. We have been married for 57 years and we are still going strong. We are soul mates. So I cannot be too hard on folks that married Mr. or Miss Wrong.

There are a lot of bad apples looking for mates. I don't believe God intended for someone to live with an abusive mate. Married women are often battered and some are killed. Some try to live through an abusive marriage. When it is divorce or live to be beaten or killed, I cannot see any other alternative but to break the marriage. If the legal system worked perfectly, these abusive husbands would be in prison and forever marked as felons. But the system is not perfect. There are some suave men that are potentially violent that can pretty much have there pick of naïve women when the choice is based on appearance or other trivial assets.

***Ephesians 5:26 "Husbands love your wives, even as Christ also loved the church and gave himself for it."***(KJV)

Of course every man knows you do not beat you wife or girlfriend and scripture really may not be needed for some. It may be that the list of things where divorce is justified should include physical and verbal abuse.

The solution that goes a long way of marrying the wrong mate is to read and follow ***2 Corinthians 6:14: "Be ye not unequally yoked together with unbelievers; for what fellowship hath righteousness with unrighteousness? And what communion hath light with darkness?"***

But I have oversimplified the problem with one scripture. What is the solution when the people involved are not Christians? Or they are the empty believers that are going to heaven but do not have a clue about being filled with the Holy Spirit.

Love, or whatever it is, can be an uncontrollable force. I can remember my crush on Joyce C in the first grade. I was destined to marry this beautiful little girl until Jack N, another first grader, said, "She is ugly." I could not be in love with an ugly girl if Jack N thought she was ugly. So my love faded for her from then on, but I recently found a picture of her in a Bible school picture at Brushy Prairie school. Joyce C is the one to the left of the teacher from the readers perspective. I am the second from the right in the picture or the fourth one to the left of the teacher. I should not have listen to Jack.

She is cute. My point in all this, there is something really strange about the forces involved when we connect with someone we end up marrying. It defies all logic and is in most cases irrational.

Of course Joyce C didn't know that I had a crush on her. I just felt the strange thing in my body about every time I looked at her. This power of love can put strange people together, and it is easy to see why people make terrible choices in mates.

## *Election:*

Here is doctrine that I could easily jump over. However, one must include all the scriptures to get at the truth. The extreme belief in election is that God picks out the people who go to heaven and ones who go to hell. For some, this is an extreme Calvinist point of view. Based on scripture, the concept of "election" will first be developed and then the broad view of "whosoever" will follow. This should keep everybody continuing to read.

The idea of election is in the Bible. Dealing first in logic; Jesus, when he started his ministry, selected the disciples. He pointed to twelve of the many followers and gave them a special place in his kingdom. It was a finger pointing episode saying "you, you, and you" will be my apostles. There were many followers in the ranks of the disciples that did not get the apostle appointment. There was nothing about the ones He picked that an ordinary person could find that was outstanding. Jesus knew their talents and courage without reading their resumes. He knew what they were capable of doing for the kingdom of God. The twelve apostles were elected. He even picked Judas deliberately. The eleven, with their hidden talent known only to Jesus, would spread the gospel. Judas, with his lack of faith in Jesus', would turn Jesus over to the Jewish authorities. It was all predestined and the twelve were elected. They really didn't know what Jesus was trying to do at first, but Jesus taught them, and they would have flunked any written test until the Holy Spirit invaded them. None of them deserved the appointment, but they were picked and had at first an easy time to inherit eternal life. Eventually, they were tried in fire.

Then there is Saul on the road to Damascus to imprison more Christians. He helped kill Stephen. He was an extremist of the Pharisee sect. He did not deserve the appointment, but God of heaven called him. It would seem grossly unfair if it was all set before birth that the elect would be the only ones saved. Go to all the scriptures to get the truth.

## *Anyone:*

**Acts 2:21 "And it shall come to pass, that whosoever shall call on the name of the Lord shall be saved."** (KJV)

## The Elect:

*Romans 9:11 "For the children being not yet born, neither having done any good or evil, that the purpose of God according to election might stand, and not of works, but of him that calleth."* (KJV)

## Anyone:

*Matthew 18:4 "Whosoever therefore shall humble himself as this little child, the same is greatest in the kingdom of heaven."* (KJV)

## The Elect:

*Isaiah 42:1 "Behold my servant, whom I uphold; mine elect, in whom my soul delighteth; I have put my spirit upon him: he shall bring forth judgment to the Gentiles."* (KJV)

The only conclusion from the author's point of view is that both "election and whosoever" exist side by side. This makes human logic. Every business owner selects talent that can be used to grow their business. Business entrepreneurs do not have the same insight into human talent as does the Holy Spirit. Election is a way to pick talent that will make things happen. Yet Christ died for all, and whosoever will may come.

What right did I have for Mary E waiting for me to convert me from being an atheist to a believer? In addition, she held Bible studies when we dated. What right did I have to see a vision of an angel on my road to Damascus, which happened at a country church? What right did I have to see all the miracles in my life? What right did I have to be so manipulated by the Holy Spirit that He became my mentor? What right did I have to speak in tongues, have visions, and to prophesy? What right did I have to want to reach the lost more than anything I do? It was God, and I was elected. That does not make me any better or any higher or anything than the smart folks that came to Jesus on their own. In fact, the "whosoever crowd" have some reason to boast of coming to Jesus without all the outside help.

If Christians would just read the entire New Testament with the help of the Holy Spirit, I believe that all the division in church would vanish. It is not a good thing when a Christian falls under the category of being a Traditionalist where they follow what their denomination says to believe. I have capitalized Traditionalist because I firmly believe it is a malady that is based on someone's background when that started a denomination, and the belief is usually a half truth.

# CHAPTER 14: HISTORY OF THE CHURCH

The Christian church was forged in the fires of false accusation, torture, and death. With a unified state religion and a governmental structure that kept every citizen under its iron grip, the Roman Empire tolerated no authority other than its own and regarded anything that resisted or opposed it as an extremely dangerous threat". Jesus warne"d his first disciples," (**Matthew 10:18, 22): "On my account you will be brought before governors and kings...All people will hate you because of me**" And so it happened and continues to happen for all who uncompromisingly followed Jesus. (KJV)

The early church up through the third century and particularly before the conversion of the emperor Constantine believed that Christians could and did live a sinless life, and they knew and were willing to accept that being a Christian could cost them their lives. Death is part of life, but we all hope to be alive when Christ returns or to at least die in our sleep. The early Christian knew that torture beyond belief awaited them prior to their death. Yet they thought it a privilege to die as a martyr for the cause of Christ. They were going through what Jesus had experienced.

The poor made up the major portion of the early church. They were in general the poor lower class of society. If the Christians belonged to the higher class of society, particularly if they were Romans, the penalty was beheading or exiled. The others were tortured to death.

The practice for the early Christians was to give all their assets to the church, and then the church would help with money and food when there was a need. Even in our modern society, there is worry about finances, and the poor of the first three centuries were as worried about their resources for survival as they were about being burned at the stake.

The Emperor Constantine was converted from Roman paganism to

Christianity. Constantine was not exactly the perfect emperor, but he was an improvement. As far as government was concerned, his conversion changed everything including the church. It started the formalization of Christianity. At least there was a respite from the horrible physical persecutions after Constantine's conversion, which would obviously be a welcome event for Christians. Maybe, however, Constantine was the beginning of the spiritual decline of the church.

Constantine was a very superstitious ruler. He was a sun worshiper and may have never stopped this practice. In reality, the sun is super important to the creation of our world. The lights that will be turned on to read this book came from the sun. The sun lighted the earth, and the leaf captured this energy storing it in trees. The trees were processed by nature into fossil fuel that is burned to create steam that is turned into work through the turbines. The turbines turn the generator that creates the electricity. The energy used by humans and other creatures come from eating stuff created by the sun. Sun worship, of course, is not proper, but at least this worship is closer to truth than worshipping idols.

Constantine's father was pro-Christian. When Constantine had a vision from heaven he was theoretically converted. Although he did not get baptized until his pending death. *"He himself appears to have been a sun worshipper, one of a number of late-pagan cults which had observances in common with Christians... they held their services on Sunday, knelt towards the East and had their nativity-feast on 25th December, the birthday of the sun at the winter solstice. Many Christians found it easy to apostatize because of this confusion; the Bishop of Troy told Julian he had always prayed secretly to the sun. Constantine never abandoned sun-worship and kept the sun on his coins. He made Sunday into a day of rest, closing the law courts and forbidding all work except agricultural labor."* Most of the sun worship has been dropped by the church except the Christmas date, and we see the outside influence on Sunday the day of worship in the Christian faith."

The point to be made is this that things can change even without basic faith that actually come from cultural things other than the Bible and the Holy Spirit.

Our further reality check of Constantine was that he had little regard for human life. He executed his eldest son, his own second wife, his favorite sister's husband and many more people. Constantine was perhaps an emperor who gave a nod to Christianity, and at best he was a nominal Christian. Change was in the wind, and this change accelerated the departure from the practice of the early church.

Even before Constantine, the church was evolving. The church in Rome was organized by 250 AD, and the church was wealthy enough to support a bishop, forty-six presbyters, seven deacons, seven sub-deacons, forty-two ministers, and fifty two exorcists. Inventories showed a vast amount of goods were seized: gold, silver, precious jewels, and supplies of food and clothing. There was mass apostasy that was lead by the bishops. Morals generally fell as time went on.

Yet, there is something about man's attempt at improving institutions that often creates the opposite effect. In government, one look at the United States of America is enough to see the trend from simple to complicated. Every alleged problem is now addressed with an agency with massive forms for the people to complete. Agencies now write laws as does the Supreme Court. Laws go from a few pages to immense works that not many can understand. In a sense, the church went from the simple to the complicated. The early church met in homes where the leadership was often uneducated. The modern sophisticated church meets in elaborate temples where the ministers were required to get college degrees and graduate from approved seminaries. The people meeting in the homes of the early church prophesied through the teaching of the Holy Spirit or spoke in tongues with interpretations. This form was replaced in the modern church with trained clergy and an order of service that was formulated and controlled.

The early Christians ate together. They supported each other financially. Basically, good or bad, there is no comparison between the early church and the developed church of today.

Proof of the church moving sometimes in an apostate fashion shows up in reformers trying to correct what they feel is wrong, and it in most cases was wrong. The church has had its share of reformers over time who tried to get back to Bible. The song "Give me that Old Time Religion" expressed some of the feeling about the evolved church. Luther, Wesley, and others were needed to attempt to put the church back on a Biblical path.

To understand what our sisters and brothers went through up until Constantine's reigned as emperor from 306 to 337 AD, a brief look at some of the Roman laws tells part of the story. Christians were pictured as lowest form of humanity. There were accusations against them that were designed to make the people of the Roman Empire hate Christians

### The Roman law stated: [xvi]

*"1 Let no one have gods of his own, neither new ones nor strange ones, but only those instituted by the State. No one may hold meetings at night in the city.*
*2 Of those who introduce new religions with unknown customs or methods by which the minds of the people could be disturbed, those of the upper classes shall be deported, and those of the lower classes shall be put to death."*

The early church was taught and believed that there was one God who created the universe. Since this was different than what the Roman Empire believed, the government incomprehensibly put a law in place to eradicate this belief. This became the basis for the persecution of Christians. The charges would include refusing to pay religious deference to the emperors. The Christians were charged with being nonreligious. They were atheists in the eyes of the Romans, Jews, and others. It was considered against the law to not pay reverence to the imperial majesties and to their genius. The Christians refused to swear by the emperors. It was high treason to be against the Roman religion. The Christians failed to celebrate the festivals of Caesars. It placed the Christian in direct opposition against the government of Rome. This put them in a precarious position from what the Bible taught of supporting all governments that they assumed God put in power. Here was a good example of when the government had gone too far, where resistance was justified.

**1 Peter 2: 13-14 "Submit yourselves to every ordinance of man for the Lord's sake: whether it be to king, as supreme; Or unto governors, as unto them that are sent by him for the punishment of evildoers, and for the praise of them that do well."** (KJV)

There is a judgment call by Christians, through the Holy Spirit, as to whether resistance is justified or not. Hitler's Germany and Japan were our nation's enemies. Both Germany and Japan were engaged in very evil activities, and these countries moved outside this scripture from **1 Peter 2: 13-14.** Resistance and war, in my opinion, can be justified.

The Christian church started under the worst possible dictatorships of Rome that required worship of the emperor and other gods. God picked this time in history to send his Son to earth. If a committee of humans would have met to decide the time, they might have decided to wait and send Christ after printing presses were invented or when the internet was up and running. The Moses religion was dominated with the

Jews, and Christianity created a strong conflict with the Jews. It had to be the best time because God picked it, but maybe man was to the limit of being able to survive as a society, and the teachings of Jesus were necessary to insure that human kind continued.

Nero, one of the emperors, at a time when the church was in its infancy, allegedly burned Rome to the ground to clear land for the palatial complex, the Domus Aurea in 64 AD. The burning was Nero's way of doing today's emanate domain. He blamed Christians for the fire.

Nero was notoriously cruel, particularly to Christians. He was comparatively cruel when compared to the emperors before and after his reign. To get a glimpse of Nero's brutality, he had his stepbrother, his two wives and his mother murdered. He reigned from 54 to 68 AD and ended his position as emperor by committing suicide.

The modern church is struggling for identity and mission. The church has redesigned its methodology, structure, and mission compared to what was described in the Bible. Evaluating this change is a personal decision. The world has changed, and perhaps the church was changing to meet the challenges of the age. However, when in search of the truth, there is a feeling of correctness by going back to what the early church believed.

The Bible stated in **Hebrews 13:8** *"**Jesus Christ the same yesterday, and today, and forever.**"* (KJV) Many Christians want what the early church had where they would be so convinced of the truth of the Bible that they could withstand the torture and death of Christians in the early church.

The canon of our Bible had not been established, and this act would hopefully solve some of the problems of the truth, but in reality it did not because people begin to pick and choose what they wanted to believe. This created denomination after denomination. So even with the present day Bible, all Christians are not on the same page. Somehow the Bible did not establish a unified belief system in some aspects. If a modern Christian does not want to get out in the streets to evangelize, she or he does not, and they often use scripture to prove that they do not want to or need to do this unpleasant task. This, in itself, slows or retards the growth of Christianity, and the Muslims can and are making converts while we as Christians look for the scripture where the words of Jesus are ignored. The words ignored are: **Acts 1:8: ""But ye shall receive power, after that the Holy ghost is come upon you , and ye shall be witnesses unto me both in Jerusalem, and in all Judaea, and in Samaria, and unto the utter most parts of the earth."** (KJV) Also statements at the end of the Gospels are discounted. Yet, we cling to **Ephesians 4:11: "And he gave some, apostles; and some, prophets; and some, evangelists; and some, pastors and teachers."** (KJV) Does this give us an excuse for letting people die and go to Hell? Absolutely not. Paul in Ephesians is saying these are the job descriptions of people inside the church. Outside we all are to do exactly what Jesus said to do. Witness. Witness. Witness.

There is also a feeling that we of the 21st century are smarter than men and women of the past, which is not true. There is a vast amount of knowledge in our modern society, but the amount of knowledge held by one individual is limited. Considering all of the modern society, there is more knowledge, but pieces of it reside in many individuals. In fact, this amount of knowledge may be constant. People in the

Bible were using iron in spears and swords. This means that a few ancient people knew how to make iron from ore. Some could navigate by the stars. A number of them could create cloth out of cotton or wool. Pick up any object around, and ask one's self how it was made. Most of the time, we do not know. Teaching college level courses in engineering, the author found that there is just so much knowledge that can be packed into a student. The limit is the human brain. Whether a student graduates from Harvard or from some lesser esteemed college, there is a maximum value of information that can be absorbed.

When I served as an expert witness in product liability cases, I usually had to prove state of art. This means that an older product could not be made safer if the solution had not been invented at the time. I often had to remind the court that America went to the moon in the 1960's. The limit switch that could have been added to unreasonably dangerous products was used on space craft 55 years ago and before. Or a patent search would reveal the safety device had a 1920 patent. Teenagers are all smarter than their parents until they reach maturity. They think this because of this concept that moderns are much smarter than ancients. Emphatically, this is false. The Bible is old, and therefore thought to be not relevant because modern people must know so much more. Looking at my world from 1934 to 2015, it appears, at least in the USA, we may not be as smart as the folks in first century.

People can punch in a text on their smart phone and send it anywhere around the world. They can buy an "app" to learn a new language on their smart cell phone, but 99% of the users of the smart phone do not know how the phone works. Unless someone somewhere had the know how to design and make the phone, the average user today would know no more than Paul of the Bible about how the technology of the cell phone actually works. Operation of a cell phone is known, but the intricate design is not known to the masses.

The truth of the Bible is evident in the growth of Christianity under persecution. *"We wage a battle when we are challenged to face the tribunals of law. There, in peril of life, we give testimony for the truth. Guards and informers bring up accusations against the Christians as sexual deviants and murderers, blasphemers and traitors, enemies of public life, desecrators of temples, and criminals against the religion of Rome. Look, you do not deal with us in accordance with the formalities of criminal cases even though you consider the Christian guilty of every crime and an enemy of the gods, emperors, laws, morals; yes, of the whole of nature.* "You do not," so they tell us, "worship the gods, nor do you make sacrifices to the emperors." *Accordingly we are charged with sacrilege and high treason. We are publicly accused of being atheists and criminals who are guilty of high treason. To begin with, those who openly confessed were arrested, and then a vast multitude was convicted on the basis of their disclosures, not so much on the charge of arson as for their hatred of the human race. Their execution was made into a game: they were covered with the skins of wild animals and torn to pieces by dogs. They were hung on crosses. They were burned, wrapped in flammable material and set on fire as darkness fell, to illuminate the night. Nero had opened his gardens for this spectacle and put on circus games. He himself mingled with the crowd dressed as a charioteer or stood up high on a chariot. Although these people were guilty and deserved the severest penalty, all this gave rise to compassion for them, for it was felt that they were being victimized, not for the public good, but to satiate the cruelty of one man."*[xvii]

Then the Roman government was not sure of the format for dealing with the early Christians. *"Gaius Pliny, governor in Asia Minor, to the Emperor Trajan: It is my custom, Sire, to report to you everything about which I am in doubt, for who could better guide my uncertainty or instruct my ignorance? I have never been present at trials of Christians; therefore I do not know what or how much to punish or to investigate.*[xviii]

*"Gaius Pliny, the governor of Asia Minor had to inquire to Emperor Trajan about how to handle the trial of Christians. He asked if age should make a difference or whether children, those of a tender age, should be treated differently. He wanted to know what the results should be when the Christian repents. He then wanted clarification as to whether the Christian should be condemned even if there was no crime. Pliny asked them three times if they were a Christian. They were then led away to death. He was essentially asking for clarification of what he was doing.*

*"There were some Roman citizens who were Christian. Gaius Pliny, the governor of Asia Minor, had questions related to the these Christians. He said they had this same madness, in other words, they believed in Christ. He also stated that this Christianity was becoming wide spread. An anonymous accusation was presented against many Christians. Pliny wanted to know if it were acceptable to acquit the people that denied being Christian, either now or before, and offered before the Emperors image incense and wine. He came prepared with the statues of the gods and incense and wine. All the accused had to do was deny Christ and present the appropriate offering to the gods.*

*"Some named by the accusers denied being Christian, and that they were Christians three years to twenty years ago, but they said they stopped being a Christian. All of these claimed to have ceased from being a Christian, and they worshiped the image of the emperor and the images of the gods. Since there was such a large number accused of being a Christian, and Christianity had spread from the cities to the villages, the governor wanted to know if he were doing things correctly.*

*"I thought it all the more necessary, then, to find out finally what was true by putting to torture two girls who were called serving girls. But I found nothing but a depraved and enormous superstition. Consequently I adjourned the investigation and now turn to you for advice".*

The defense offered by some was to tell the governor what they did in their worship service. The totality of their guilt or error was what they simply did in their worship service. They met on fixed day before daylight. <u>They alternated who performed in the service.</u> They sang a hymn, took an oath to not commit a crime such as theft, robbery, adultery, and not break their word. They parted company and then met together to share a meal.

Trajan's replay to Gaius Pliny was that he handled the situation correctly. The Emperor stated that anonymous accusation were inadmissible in the criminal trials. If they denied Christ, worship the Emperor and the gods, they could be released.

Polycarp's execution tells much about the faith of the Christians and the manner in which he died. " *They tortured two young slaves and one of them under torture revealed the location of Polycarp.*

"The constable took the one young slave along with mounted armed men to search for Polycarp. They found him on a Friday evening in an upper room in a small cottage. The search party was amazed at his age and composure. He immediately took care of his captures physical needs by providing food and drink. He asked them for one hour of undisturbed prayer. During this hour he had a vision of his pillow being on fire. He knew that he would be burned to death. He left with armed party riding on a donkey into the city. Herod, the chief of police, and his father rode out to meet Polycarp who got into their carriage. They urged him to save his life by meeting the requirements of Emperor worship and offering to the idols. They urged him to save his life by doing this meaningless thing. They said, "What is wrong with saying 'Lord!' and 'Caesar!' and sacrificing, and the rest of it, and thereby saving your life?

"At first Polycarp did not answer them. Finally to get some peace from their continued badgering him, he said, "I am not willing to do what you advise me."

"Even the spectators pitied and bewailed them. The noble martyrs of Christ attained such towering strength of soul that not one of them uttered a cry or groan.

"In the same way they endured fearful torment when they were condemned to the wild beasts. They were rolled over shells and were subjected to all kinds of other tortures, for the tyrant hoped to induce them to deny their faith by the prolonged torture, if that were possible.

"The infernal Tempter used many devices against them, but thanks be to the Lord he was powerless against them all. The noble Germanicus strengthened the weakness of others by his steadfastness. He wrestled gallantly with the wild beasts.

*When the proconsul tried to persuade him, saying that he had pity on his youth, he forcibly pulled the wild beast towards himself, wishing to be freed more quickly from this godless and unjust life. The whole mob, horrified at the heroism of the God-loving and God-fearing Christian sect, shouted, "Away with the atheists! Get moving! Look for Polycarp!*

*"Only one man, a certain Quintus from Phrygia, who had just recently come from there, turned coward when he saw the wild beasts. He was the one who had voluntarily given himself up to the court and had also persuaded some others to do the same. After earnest entreaty the proconsul persuaded him to take the oath and to sacrifice. Therefore, brothers, we do not find it praiseworthy if some of us voluntarily give ourselves up. The Gospel does not teach this. But Polycarp, in contrast, when he first heard of all this, acted admirably by showing no fear... When they did not find him, they arrested two young slaves, one of whom became a traitor under torture.*

*"Taking the young slave with them, the constables set out against him on Friday at evening with a squadron of mounted men and their usual arms. Late in the evening they came upon him and found him in an upper room of a small cottage...They were amazed at his great age and his calm dignity...He immediately ordered food and drink to be served them, as much as they wanted, and he asked them to give him an hour for undisturbed prayer...And when the moment of departure came, they seated him on a donkey and in this way brought him into the city.*

*"It was a great Sabbath. Herod, the chief of police, and Nicetes, his father, rode to meet him. They took him into their carriage and sitting next to him urged him by saying, "What is*

wrong with saying 'Lord!' and 'Caesar!' and sacrificing, and the rest of it, and thereby saving your life?

"At first he did not answer them, but when they did not leave him in peace he said, "I am not willing to do what you advise me."...When he entered the arena there was such a tremendous uproar that nobody could be understood. When he was led forward, the proconsul asked him if he was Polycarp.

"This he affirmed. The proconsul wanted to persuade him to deny his faith, urging him, "Consider your great age," and all the other things they usually say in such cases. "Swear by the genius of the emporers.

"When Polycarp got into the arena the crowd was screaming and mad with demonic control. Polycarp raised his hand over them and looked up in Heaven and said, 'Away with the atheists'."

The proconsul continued to try and save his life. He simple told him to *"Swear and I will release you! Curse Christ."*

Polycarp told the proconsul that for 86 years he had served Christ. "He could not blaspheme his King and Savior. He stated that he had served the Lord, and He has never done him any harm. He just could not do what the proconsul requested."

"The proconsul did not give up. He asked Polycarp, "Swear by the genius of Caesar," Polycarp then confessed again that he was a Christian.

"Polycarp asked the proconsul if he wanted to learn about what Christianity is to set a time where he could explain the gospel to him.

*"The proconsul asked Polycarp to convince the crowd that Christianity was a good thing. He stated, "Try to persuade the people."*

Polycarp's answer was, *"You I consider worthy that I should give an explanation, for we have been taught to pay respect to governments and authorities appointed by God as long as it does us no harm. But as to that crowd, I do not consider them worthy of my defense."*

The proconsul told Polycarp that he had wild beasts, and that he would have him thrown into the arena with the wild beasts.

Polycarp just declared to *"Let them come"*. He was not frighten by them. He was not willing to go from better to worst.

The proconsul was angered. *"He told Polycarp that he belittle the beasts and if he did not change his mind he would him thrown into the fire."*

Polycarp replied that the threat of fire on the earth for a short time was better than eternity in hell where the fire was never quenched. This old man was full of courage and joy. His face showed the joy of the Holy Spirit. He basically said to get on with it. None of the threats moved him. He was the image of Jesus as he faced his demise.

*"The proconsul sent his herald into the arena three times to announce to the crowd that Polycarp was a Christian. This enraged the people. The pagans and the Jews were screaming at the top of their voices. They wanted the officials to turn a lion loose on Polycarp. Philip, a high priest of public worship, explained that this was not allowed because the wild beast contests had been closed. Then there arose a unanimous shout*

that Polycarp should be burned alive." The crowd rushed out to find fire wood. They piled the wood and brush from the public baths, workshop, and where ever they could find it. The Jews were particularly energetic in finding material to burn Polycarp to death.

"The logs and brush were piled around a post that was sunken in the ground. The officials were going to nail Polycarp to the post, but he said it was not necessary. Polycarp said "Let me be. He who gives me the strength to endure the fire will also give me the strength to remain at the stake unflinching, without the security of your nails. ...When he had spoken the Amen and finished his prayer, the executioners lit the fire. Polycarp was a marvelous witness to Christ in his martyrdom."

Polycarp's testimony actually screamed by the pagans and Jews was that : "He is the teacher of Asia! The father of the Christians! The destroyer of our gods! He has persuaded many not to sacrifice and not to worship. As a Christian let us hope that at our memorial service that we might be accused of the same alleged crimes that were committed by Polycarp.... he had the body put in the middle of the pyre and burned, according to their custom. So afterwards we were able to take up his bones, more valuable than jewels and more precious than gold, and to lay them to rest in our burying place. There we will come together as often as God will grant us, in jubilation and joy, as much as we are able. There we will celebrate the anniversary of his martyrdom and death like a birthday, in memory of those who have fought and won the fight before, and for the strengthening and preparation of those who still have to face it. Such is our report about the blessed Polycarp who, counting those from Philadelphia, was the twelfth to suffer martyrdom at Smyrna."

*" The proconsul went to Pergamum in Asia Minor.* **Carpus** *and* **Papylus** *were brought to the proconsul. The proconsul questioned them asking Carpus his name. The answer was that his first name was Christian and his name in the world was Carpus. The proconsul stated they knew the decrees of the Emperor. He reminded them that they must worship all the gods. He told them to come front and center and sacrifice as was necessary.*

*Carpus replied, "I am a Christian. I honor Christ, the son of God, who has come in the latter times to save us and has delivered us from the madness of the Devil. I will not sacrifice to such idols. Do what you please. It is impossible for me to offer sacrifices to these delusive phantoms, these demons, for they who sacrifice to them become like them...*

*" Both of you, sacrifice to the gods and listen to reason!"*

*"The proconsul said, "You must sacrifice; the Caesar has commanded it."*

*Carpus answered, "The living do not sacrifice to the dead."*

The proconsul asked, *"Do you believe that the gods are dead?"*

Carpus replied, *"If you would like to know, they were never even men, nor did they ever live that they could die. Believe me, you are caught up in a grave delusion."*

The proconsul replied, *"I have let you talk too much nonsense and thus have misled you to blaspheme the gods and the majesty. You shall not continue in this way. You will sacrifice or else – ! What do you say?"*

Carpus said, *"I cannot sacrifice. I have never yet sacrificed to* idols."

"The proconsul ordered Carpus to be hung up and with the tools of torture until his skin was essentially removed, and Carpus cried out again and again, "I am a Christian! I am a Christian! I am a Christian!" After this torture had gone on for a long time he lost his strength and could not speak any more."

The proconsul therefore turned his attention from Carpus to Papylus and asked him, *"Are you a councilor?"*

He answered, *"I am a citizen.*

The proconsul asked, *"Of what city?"*

Papylus answered, *"Thyatira."*

The proconsul asked, *"Do you have any children?"*

Papylus replied, *"Oh yes, many of them, through God."*

One of the surrounding crowd shouted, "He means he has children by his Christian faith."

The proconsul shouted at him, *"Why do you lie, saying that you have children?"*

Papylus answered, *"Will you understand that I am not lying but saying the truth? In every district and city I have children in God."*

The proconsul said, *"You will sacrifice or else – ! What do you say?"*

Papylus answered, *"I have served God since my youth. I have never sacrificed to idols. I am a Christian. You cannot learn* anything else from me. There is nothing I can say which is greater or more wonderful than this." Then he also was hung up and his body was flayed with three pairs of iron instruments of torture. He did not utter a sound, but as a courageous fighter he endured the rage of the tempter.

"When the proconsul saw their outstanding steadfastness, he ordered him to be burned alive.

"They descended into the amphitheater with brisk steps, that they might be freed from this world as quickly as possible. Papylus was the first to be nailed to the stake. When the flames leaped up he prayed quietly and gave up his soul. Carpus was nailed on after him. He was full of joy...When he had spoken and the fire was burning, he prayed, "Praise be to thee O Lord, Jesus Christ, son of God, that thou didst deem me, a sinner, also worthy of this part in thee!" After these words he gave up his soul. **Agathonica** was present when these things happened. She saw the glory of the Lord which Carpus had seen and described. In this she recognized a call from heaven and raised her voice straight away. "This meal has been prepared for me. I must partake in it. I must receive the meal of glory.[xix]

"The people cried out, *"Have pity on your son."* Agathonica joyfully answered, "He has God who can care for him, for he is the provider for all. But I, why do I stand here?" She threw off her clothes and jubilantly allowed herself to be nailed to the stake.

Those standing by burst into tears and cried, "A cruel sentence! What unjust orders!"

"But she, standing erect and caught by the fire, cried out three times, "Lord, Lord, Lord, help me, for I flee unto thee." Then she gave up her soul and was perfected with the saints.

"Rusticus, the city prefect, said to Justin before the judgment seat, "First of all trust the gods and obey the Emperor."

**Justin** answered, *"Obedience to the words of our Savior Jesus Christ does not call for blame or condemnation."*

City Prefect Rusticus asked, *"Which branch of knowledge do you study?"*

Justin answered, *"I endeavored to acquaint myself with all systems. In the end I surrendered to the true teachings of the Christians. These teachings do not please those who are caught up in false beliefs."*

City Prefect Rusticus answered, *"And you enjoy the teachings of these people, you utterly wretched man?"*

Justin replied, *"The worship of the God of the Christians consists in our belief in the one God...who has made and brought forth the whole creation, visible and invisible; and in the Lord Jesus Christ whom the prophets foretold in this way: He would appear to the human race as the herald of salvation and the proclaimer of precious truth. Being only a man, I feel too insignificant to say anything appropriate about his boundless divinity. I do however acknowledge a prophetic power. He whom I have called here the son of God has been proclaimed before- hand. I know that through inspiration from God the prophets foretold his future coming to men."*

City Prefect Rusticus asked, *"Where do you assemble?"*

Justin answered, *"Where each one wants to and is able to. You *probably believe that we all come together in one and the same place. This is not so, for the God of the Christians is not limited to any one place. He fills heaven and earth. He is honored*

City Prefect Rusticus said, *"Answer, where do you assemble, or in what place do you gather your followers?"*

Justin answered, *"I live up on the hill, close to the baths of Timothy; during all this time (and I am now living in Rome for the second time) I have not known any other meeting place. I communicated the teachings of truth to anyone who wished to see me there."*

Rusticus asked, *"You still insist that you are a Christian?"* Justin answered, *"I am a Christian."* The city prefect turned to **Chariton**. *"Now you tell me, are you also a Christian?"*

Chariton answered, *"I am a Christian by the will of God."*

The city prefect now asked the woman Charito, *"What do you say, Charito?"* Charito answered, *"I am a Christian by the gift of God."*

Rusticus turned to **Euelpistus**. *"Tell me, what are you?"*

Euelpistus, a slave of the Emperor, answered, *"I, too, am a Christian; through Christ I have been freed, and by the gift of Christ I share the same hope."*

The city prefect asked **Hierax**, *"And you are a Christian too?"*

Hierax answered, *"Yes, I am a Christian, for my homage and worship belong to the same God.*

"Rusticus, the city prefect, asked, "Did Justin make you Christians too?"

Hierax replied, "I was a Christian, and I will be a Christian."

**Paeon**, who was not among the accused and was standing by, said, "I, too, am a Christian."

City Prefect Rusticus asked, *"Who taught you?"*

Paeon said, "From our parents we accepted this wonderful confession."

Euelpistus said, "I heard the words of Justin with joy. But I also learned to be a Christian from my parents."

Rusticus, the city prefect, asked, "Where are your parents?"

*Euelpistus said, "In Cappadocia [Asia Minor].*

"Rusticus also asked **Hierax**, "Who are your parents?"

He answered, "Christ is our true father, and our faith in him is our mother. My earthly parents died. I was taken away from Iconium in Phrygia [Asia Minor], and from there I came here."

The city prefect, Rusticus, turned to **Liberian**. "What do you say now? Are you a Christian too? Are you also godless?

Liberian answered, "I, too, am a Christian, for I worship and give homage to the only true God."

The city prefect now turned once more to Justin. "Listen, you who are called a learned man. You think that you possess true insight; if you should be scourged and beheaded, do you believe you will ascend into heaven?"

*Justin answered, "I believe that if I endure these things I shall have what he promises. For I know that the divine gift will stay with all who live this way until the end of the world."*

*City Prefect Rusticus said, "Do you suppose, then, that you will ascend into heaven and receive some reward there?"*

*Justin said, "I do not suppose it; I know it. I am certain of it."*

*City prefect, Rusticus, said, "We have to come now finally to the matter in hand. It is getting urgent. Come here and with one accord offer a sacrifice to the gods."*

*Justin answered, "No right-thinking person slanders communion with God by going to godlessness."*

*Rusticus, the city prefect, said, "Unless you obey, you will be mercilessly punished."*

*Justin answered, "It is our wish to be martyred for the sake of our Lord Jesus Christ and so be saved. This will be our salvation and our confidence at the much more fearful judgment seat of our Lord and Savior, who will demand that the whole world come before his forum."*

*So also said the other martyrs, "Do what you will, for we are Christians and do not sacrifice to idols."*

*Then Rusticus, the city prefect, pronounced sentence: "These people, who have refused to sacrifice to the gods and do not obey the command of the Emperor, shall be scourged and taken away to be beheaded according to the laws."*

*"Even the blessed **Pothinus**, the overseer of the church at Lugdunum, who had reached the great age of more than ninety years, was dragged before the tribunal. He was physically so feeble that he was scarcely able to breathe, but he was strong with inward joy and full*

*of longing for the crown of martyrdom. His body was tired to death because of his great age and his physical ailments, but his soul was kept in him so powerfully that Christ was to triumph through him. He was led before the tribunal by soldiers accompanied by the city authorities. A great multitude yelled and shouted in a wild uproar. It happened in just the same way as when Christ was condemned. He gave a good witness.*

When the governor asked him, "Who is the god of the Christians?"

He answered, "If you were worthy you would know."

"Thereupon he was ill-treated in the most merciless way. Those closest to him pounded him and kicked him viciously from all sides, not respecting his old age in the slightest. Those further away hurled at him whatever came into their hands. Scarcely breathing any more Pothinus was thrown into prison, and after two days he gave up his soul.

"**Maturus, Sanctus, Blandina, and Attalus** were taken to the wild beasts in the amphitheater, to give the pagan crowd which was gathered there a public spectacle of inhumanity. They ran the gauntlet of whips. They were already used to this. They let themselves be dragged around and mauled by the wild beasts. Everything the raving, yelling mob wanted, now from this side, now from that, they endured. They sat upon the iron chair which roasted their bodies so that the fumes rose up. Yet they heard nothing from Sanctus beyond the confession of faith he had repeated over and over again from the beginning. When they were still found alive in spite of the terrible and prolonged torture, they were finally killed. Blandina was hung on a post, delivered up to the wild beasts for food. Hung up like this in the shape of the Cross, she could be seen from afar, and through her ardent prayers she aroused increased zeal in those who were fighting, for during this fight they saw with their own eyes, right in and through the person of their sister, the one who was crucified for them. In this way it was shown to all who *believe in him that everyone who suffers for the glory of Christ is always in fellowship with the living God. As none of the wild beasts had yet touched Blandina, she was taken down from the post and thrown into prison once more, to be kept ready for a new fight.*

*"Most of those who had denied their faith were received back into the bosom of the church. The fire of their lives was rekindled and burned brightly. They learned to confess and stood before the tribunal again, full of life and vigor, once more to be plagued by the governor. In the meantime the command of the Emperor had arrived: those who denied their faith should be set free; the others should be executed.*

The great festival had just begun. Large numbers of people had flocked together from many faraway places. Before the eyes of the crowd the governor had all the blessed ones conducted to the tribunal in a ceremonial procession. Again he started to examine them. All those who clearly possessed Roman citizenship were beheaded. The rest were sent to the wild beasts. Christ was glorified magnificently by those who had formerly denied him. The pagans could not grasp it. They gave witness. **Attalus** sat in the iron chair. His body burned. The fumes rose up. On being asked, "What is God's name?" he answered, "God does not have a name as a man has.

The conclusion of reading some of the history of the early Christians who were martyrs is that it would be very difficult to find Christians today who could boastfully say, "Yah I could stand that." From the martyr perspective there is a big difference between the early Christians and the Christians of the 21$^{st}$ century. This an important fact. Things have changed in the Christian faith. I marvel at their courage, and their support of the Gospel. Each martyr should reinforce our belief in the Gospel of Jesus Christ. This suffering cannot be made up. It happens only in the convicting truth of Jesus Christ. Maybe there will be a revolution of the Christian faith that will carry us weak and half committed Christian to become like the early Church.

The early Christians are part of the story, but the rest of the historical story of the Christian church needs to be told. We cannot think about change unless we believe that the modern church has failed in its mission. We must believe one sentence: "There is more!".

Examination of the early Catholic church leadership should suffice to prove there was a distinct decrease in following what Christ taught. After the reformation, the churches did improve. There is still more.

I wish that I could avoid this next segment of looking at the fallen popes, but my intent is to lock into the argument that the church only lasted a couple hundred year before there was a steep decline in spirituality. The Reformation by Martin Luther came, but it did not go far enough. The revivals came but did not continue for long. There are some awesome modern churches, but there are way too many churches that are dead and ineffective. There is a big emphasis on fellowship, clever powerless preaching, and a total lack of evangelism. Once in awhile, some desperate sinner stumbles into these churches and finds Christ.

It is my opinion that there were and still are fully committed Christian throughout history. It is not hopeless, but if we do not recognize that there truly is more and that political and social things in the USA must change, it will be hopeless. We can change presidents, but we have to change the people. That can only come through the power of the Holy Spirit. This is my hope.

## The Pope Table[xx]

| Pope Leo X  (1513 to 1521) | A person paid money for their sins to be forgiven. * |
|---|---|
| Pope Julius II  (1513 to 1531) | He had an illegitimate daughter, and had several |

|  | mistresses.* |
| --- | --- |
| Pope Alexander VI (1492 to 1503) | He had several mistresses and one illegitimate daughter. * |
| Pope Benedict IX (1032 to 1048) | Accused of rape and murders. Described as immoral.* |
| Pope John XII (955 to 964) | Murdered, mutilation, arson. Palace was a whorehouse. * |
| Pope Stephen VI (896 to (897) | Dug up a cadaver and held a trial. Was eventually arrested and locked in a dungeon.* |
|  | * All the above are alleged accusations. Reader verify. |

The present Catholic Church is, on a whole, no different than all the protestant churches. The past history does not define them today. In Siloam Springs, Arkansas there was a Monsignor who possessed all the gifts of the Holy Spirit, and he had a large following of Pentecostal Christians. It is not as simple as this is bad and that is good. Bad and good churches are ubiquitous. Attendees beware!

# CHAPTER 15: CLOSURE

I hope that it becomes clear to the Christians that there is a need to change the church by going back to the truth of Jesus Christ. If there were persecution today, the church of Jesus Christ would become a minority in the USA overnight. Many would denounce the Lord.

We complain constantly about government. Not even the Supreme Court protects America from its terrible sins. The court once supported owning slaves. They supported removing prayer from schools. They supported pornography being distributed. They supported abortions. Now they support same sex marriage. Hollywood produces films that shock the Christians and infuriates the Muslims. Other problems exist in the world that Christians tolerate. The politicians have a stock answer: "I agree with you, and we are working on that problem in congress." Of course they have been working on the problem forever without success.

There are allegedly 229,157,250 Christians in the United States. It can be assumed that many in this group will not be Christian by the Bible's definition of Christianity. If 10 percent would produce one convert of this vast number per year in ten years there would be twice as many Christians as there are today.

There are many problems that have prevented Christian culture from influencing the USA. One of them is the way Christians conduct services. The average church functions as a place where the Christians can do only limited work in the church, and this trains them to do nothing. Most of that activity does not involve evangelism, but instead focuses on good things like feeding and clothing the poor as one example. When this is done without evangelism, there is only a short term help for the poor. I went to a "laundry love" program where the church gave quarters for the people's wash and provided free pizza, but no one was telling the recipients why they were doing this. In other words, there was no evangelism. My church, Grace Point in Springdale, Arkansas, has free breakfast for the homeless people at a fast food restaurant. They do have a Christian message and a ride to church. We must do church seven days a week to see significant change.

As I wrote this book, I turned and saw the following view on my wall. The real scene said to me that this is where many Christians are at. They are on the wall and not being used.

Churches have many people that can be used outside the church to win men, women, boys, and girls to Christ. Maybe it takes more confidence in people by the pastors than what they normally have. Maybe some pastors have fear of losing control. Maybe there is a fear of have the untrained run-off some of their congregation. Whatever this reluctance to using the people in the church should end. There is little to lose and much to gain. Church should be run as it is described in 1Corinthians 14 without the limitation put on women. This was a specific church with a specific problem. Phillip in Acts 21: 9 clearly states that Phillip's four daughters prophesied and that is done in churches. Why everyone is skipping 1 Corinthians 14: 29-32 to what we have today with many not allowing women to participate fully is beyond belief. Here are the scriptures again:

*1 Corinthians 14: 29-32 "Let the prophets speak two or three, and let the other judge. If any thing be revealed to another that sitteth by, let the first hold his peace. For ye may all prophesy one by one that all may learn, all may be comforted. And the spirits of the prophets are subject to the prophets."*

*1 Corinthians 14: 34 "Let your women keep silence in the church for it is not permitted unto them to speak:"*

*Acts 21:9 "And the same man (Philip the evangelist) had four daughters, virgins, which did prophesy."*

Then of course there is the opinion by many that a person gets all there is to get when he or she is saved. Again the scripture that at least should make a Christian think that maybe there is more than the baptism of repentance.

Again reading the scripture where the twelve people believed in the Lord, but they had not heard that there was a Holy Spirit. Read this one more time and realize THERE IS ALWAYS MORE!

*Acts 19: 1-7 [1] "And it came to pass that while Apollos was at Corinth, Paul having passed through the upper coast came to Ephesus: and finding certain disciples, [2] He said unto them, Have ye received the Holy Ghost since ye believed? And they said unto him, We have not so much as heard whether there be any Holy Ghost. [3] And he said unto them, Unto what then were ye baptized? And they said, Unto John's baptism. [4] Then said Paul,*

*John verily baptized with the baptism of repentance, saying unto the people, that they should believe on him which should come after him, that is on Christ Jesus. [5] When they heard this,* (KJV)

*they were baptized in the name of the Lord Jesus. [6] And when Paul had laid his hands upon them, the Holy Ghost came on them; and they spake with tongues and prophesied. [7] And all the men were about twelve."* (KJV)

It is the author's belief that there is more to the Christian faith than what is typically practiced. There are hurting people that need to be set free, and it will not happen unless the church as a whole changes. We need a revolution in the Christian faith to go back to what it was in the first 200 years after Christ rose from the dead. It is my prayer that some of the readers of this book will walk into an alcoholic or drug addict's home and point their finger in love at some poor lost wretch living in hell and going to an eternity in a worse hell and tell this one Christ died for him or her. As Reverend C said to my Dad four words. "Leonard, you need Jesus." Dad said as he cried, "I know I need Jesus." Go and do it!

# ABOUT THE AUTHOR

The author's life started in a small town in Mongo, Indiana. It was a beautiful place in northeast Indiana with the Pigeon River reservoir within the village. The author lived in a small white house less than 100 feet from the reservoir's shore. His family members were in general dysfunctional. His father was an alcoholic and his mother was going to reform her husband with heated arguments. He and his sisters escaped from the home as soon as graduating from high school to search for a better life. During those very hard years, the author became an atheist.

People need to be prejudiced against somebody or some people to build themselves up. Since there were no minorities in LaGrange County, the folks designated towns as their target of prejudice. The author happened to be born in a town that was considered by the rest of the county as a village for inferior people. It was not, and in fact most of the inferior people were living in some of the towns considered the place where the elite lived. When the town hero Merlyn Wilson was killed in the 82$^{nd}$ airborne in WWII the village mourned, and young men enlisted in the military. His high school graduation class of just 8 boys and no girls enlisted in the military during the Korean war. The author was in the Navy and sailed on the USS Tercel, an old WWII minesweeper. Seeing how well the officers lived as compared to the enlisted men, He decided to go to college. He graduated with a BSME from Trine University, from the University of Toledo with an MSME, and he graduated with a PhD in engineering from Michigan State. It was all engineering, but one professor in English said he should write. Not that he could ace English exams, but the instructor liked his stories. Hopefully the readers of this book will like his true stories.

He founded businesses, and founded Earth Mission and Acts One Eight International, two active non-profit organizations to reach the lost of this world. There is little satisfaction in bench warming church pews. It is his hope that the reader will consider going into world and being the church. It actually is fun working with the Holy Spirit in evangelizing and making disciples.

He eventually had a dramatic Christian conversion and went from an atheist to a born again believer in a matter of minutes through a vision. This book is a collection of some of these stories of the Holy Spirit working in the lives of people. His goal is to take as many people with him to God's throne in heaven as possible. He has co-authored a best selling textbook on solar energy, a number of product manuals for lawyers involved in product liability that were co-authored with his son John Ryan, and a Christian novel called Exit 59 that is geared for non-Christians with a Holy Spirit conversion of the protagonist.

He is a critic of the Traditional Christian who refuses to be involved in evangelism. He knows of the suffering of sinners and how Christ can release them from bondage as happened with his entire family.

## RECOMMENDED READING

- "Surprised by the Voice of God" by Dr. Jack Deere
- "The God I never knew" by Robert Morris
- "The Happiest People on Earth" by Demos Shakarian
- "The Early Christian in Their Own Words", Eberhard Arnold, by Plough Publishing House, **www.ploughbooks.co.uk**
- "Deeper Experiences of Famous Christian", by James Gilchrist Lawson
- Go to **www.actsoneeightinternational.com**

[i] Jesus Calling, Sarah Young, Thomas Nelson, Nashville, September 2, Page 257,

[ii] King James Bible (All Bible quotes from the King James Version)

[iii] The Oxford American Dictionary and Language Guide , Oxford University Press.

[iv] Accident Statistic, National Safety Council

[v] Endnotes, Robert Frost

[vi] King James Bible

[vii] Internet source infographic site:

[viii] Wikipedia

[x] History of Christianity, by Paul Johnson, page 49, a Touchstone Book, Simon & Schuster, New York

[xi] Dr. James Mitchell Ryan MD

[xiii] Paper presented at John Brown U. 2015 by Judah D. Ryan

[xiv] Paper presented at John Brown U. 2015 by Judah D. Ryan

[xv] Hand written by Jack Apple Grandfather of the deceased girls.

[xvi] The Early Christians in their own Words, Eberhard Arnold, by Plough Publishing House, www.ploughbooks.co.uk

[xvii] The Early Christian in Their Own Words, Eberhard Arnold, by Plough Publishing House, www.ploughbooks.co.uk

[xviii] The Early Christian in Their Own Words, Eberhard Arnold, by Plough Publishing House, www.ploughbooks.co.uk

[xix] The Early Christian in Their Own Words, Eberhard Arnold, by Plough Publishing House, www.ploughbooks.co.uk

[xx] Wikipedia "Bad Popes" ; www.oddee.com/item_96537.aspx